Bandy

Marcia Croce Martin

© Copyright 2005 Marcia Croce Martin.
All rights reserved. No part of this publication may be reproduced, stored in a retrieval system, or transmitted, in any form or by any means, electronic, mechanical, photocopying, recording, or otherwise, without the written prior permission of the author.

Cover design and layout by Fletch Brendan Good
Cover photograph by Marcia Croce Martin
Back cover photograph by Stephanie Foster of *The Cape Codder*

Note for Librarians: a cataloguing record for this book that includes Dewey Decimal Classification and US Library of Congress numbers is available from the Library and Archives of Canada. The complete cataloguing record can be obtained from their online database at:
www.collectionscanada.ca/amicus/index-e.html
ISBN 1-4120-4289-5
Printed in Victoria, BC, Canada

TRAFFORD

Offices in Canada, USA, Ireland, UK and Spain
This book was published *on-demand* in cooperation with Trafford Publishing. On-demand publishing is a unique process and service of making a book available for retail sale to the public taking advantage of on-demand manufacturing and Internet marketing. On-demand publishing includes promotions, retail sales, manufacturing, order fulfilment, accounting and collecting royalties on behalf of the author.
Book sales for North America and international:
Trafford Publishing, 6E–2333 Government St.,
Victoria, BC V8T 4P4 CANADA
phone 250 383 6864 (toll-free 1 888 232 4444)
fax 250 383 6804; email to orders@trafford.com
Book sales in Europe:
Trafford Publishing (UK) Ltd., Enterprise House, Wistaston Road Business Centre, Wistaston Road, Crewe, Cheshire
CW2 7RP UNITED KINGDOM
phone 01270 251 396 (local rate 0845 230 9601)
facsimile 01270 254 983; orders.uk@trafford.com
Order online at:
www.trafford.com/robots/04-2096.html

10 9 8 7 6 5 4 3

To Lela, who instantaneously acquired a friend for life the day she called my goose a "*good little man*", and without whose intervention this story would have too sad an ending to even be told.

Table of Contents

	Introduction	1
Chapter 1:	The Stuff That Dreams Are Made Of	7
Chapter 2:	The Band	13
Chapter 3:	Making Friends	17
Chapter 4:	Coyotes in the 'Hood	23
Chapter 5:	A Christmas Miracle	29
Chapter 6:	Heartbreak	33
Chapter 7:	Birds of a Feather?	39
Chapter 8:	Premonition	47
Chapter 9:	A Friend in Need	53
Chapter 10:	A Friend, Indeed	59
Chapter 11:	There's No Place Like Home	67
Chapter 12:	Empty Nest Syndrome	71
Chapter 13:	Goose Abuse!	75
Chapter 14:	Where Do You Wander?	77
Chapter 15:	The Green, Green Grass of Home	83
Chapter 16:	The Way is Never Long	87
Chapter 17:	That Old North Wind	97
Chapter 18:	CSI: Harwich	105
Chapter 19:	A Day in the Life	109
Chapter 20:	A Honker for a Tutor	115
	Acknowledgments	125

Introduction

Even in the towns surrounding Ansonville, North Carolina, stories were circulating. The year was 1953. Lockhart Gaddy, known for his love of Canada geese, had been laid to rest. Each year thousands of wild geese made their journey from the far reaches of the north down to the hills surrounding his home.

Mr. Gaddy had not always been a goose enthusiast. Once a waterfowl hunter and a keeper of live decoys, he and a friend would await the arrival of the unsuspecting birds, then blast them out of the air en masse.

"He *murdered* those geese," exclaimed Ed McBride, whose family owned the tobacco farm abutting the Gaddy's property.

Now 82 years old, McBride was a boy at the time, and remembers catching catfish in a nearby creek and releasing them into the pond owned by Mr. Gaddy. "Gaddy's Goose Pond", as it was called, was enlarged almost yearly. Initially, his thought was to provide a nice place for his mother-in-law to fish, a pastime she enjoyed.

In 1935, the federal government ordered the release of all live decoys, a subject which we will delve into in this book, and thousands were set free, including the ones kept by Mr. Gaddy. The problem was, many of them were crippled and, though they could still fly, they didn't leave with the rest of the northbound geese. Lockhart and his good wife Hazel decided that the convalescing geese needed help, so they assumed the role of caregivers to the pitiful group that had served Mr. Gaddy in his sporting days. As they did so, they came to the realization that these geese were smart, sensitive, and individual in their personalities, and even in their looks. They began giving the geese names and could readily tell them apart.

In the fall when the migrating geese returned, the Gaddys began seeing them in a different light. They had noticed that geese liked corn by the fact that they would strip the crops in the cornfields, something that in the past had been a source of aggravation to them. Now Mr. Gaddy bought corn and fed it to the geese, and their numbers grew steadily until it was estimated that there were upwards of 10,000 geese on the hillside and at the ever enlarging pond. People came from surrounding areas to see and feed the geese. Busloads of children would visit Gaddy's Goose Pond on field trips.

Eventually Mr. Gaddy renamed his pond, "Gaddy's Wild Goose Refuge", and he constructed a small building, about ten feet by twenty feet, to house corn for his geese. He began selling cans of it at ten cents a can and many people, including the schoolchildren, came from miles away to participate in this wildlife experience.

Then one day Lockhart Gaddy came to his goose pond no more. At least not in living form. His final request was to be buried down by the pond, which was about a half-mile from his house, near to the geese he had come to know and love.

During his funeral something unique and phenomenal happened. As the minister was retelling the life of a man who had made his mark, a large formation of geese flew in and circled the outdoor gathering three times, then flew away.

Ed McBride was at his neighbor's funeral and doesn't remember much else, but he does remember the geese who made their appearance.

An elderly and distinguished Cape Codder by the name of Bill McClennan worked in nearby Albemarle at the time. He told me that for years the townspeople were abuzz about Lockhart Gaddy's funeral and the perceived keen sensitivity exhibited by the geese.

In stark contrast to his hunting days, Lockhart underwent such a transformation that he was influential in the government's decision to set aside PeeDee National Wildlife Refuge as a place where goose hunting is prohibited and the waterfowl can be assured a safe retreat. The 8,000 plus acre park is located in Anson and Richmond Counties and is about three miles from the old Gaddy and McBride homesteads, as the goose flies.

Hazel outlived Lockhart by nineteen years. She died in 1972 and was buried at the goose pond beside her husband. The geese have since all but disappeared from the pond, but the people of Ansonville are launching an effort to bring the geese and the visitors back to their town. You see, not everybody dislikes geese.

Rats with wings? Destroyers of the landscape? Fun to shoot? Indistinguishable clones? Maybe you have held some of the above sentiments about geese. If so, it is my hope that as you read the following story about a unique individual, a goose named Bandy that I call my friend, perhaps with Mr. Gaddy, you, too, will have a change of heart. If you have thought that geese were just black and white, prepare to meet one colorful and beloved gander.

Hazel Gaddy with her geese

Not one sparrow can fall to the ground without your Father knowing it.

Matthew 10:29
The Living Bible

ONE

The Stuff That Dreams Are Made Of

As a small child growing up on Cape Cod I had a passion for the local pond and all of the wild creatures it sustained. I may not remember a lot of my childhood in detail, but I do remember everything I caught, and I'm not referring to measles or mumps. My sister, being the oldest, was the head of the neighborhood wildlife club. She awarded points for whatever cool living thing we could capture and present to her. Snakes, in particular, excited me. I would capture them using a "y" shaped stick, and then grasp them behind the head to pick them up. One day I was fascinated by a ringed snake and, due to the fact that it was in the water, I ignored the proper way to handle it.

It made its way under a lilly pad and I grabbed the whole thing. I got the snake, alright—fangs in hand and all! Fortunately, it wasn't poisonous.

My highest scoring catch was an eel that I caught with my bare hands. My catch was aided, no doubt, by the fact that the eel was logy due to a mass pond poisoning, termed "shocking" the pond. I had received no verbal warnings and was oblivious to the "Keep Out Of Water!" signs, complete with skull and crossbones, posted around Long Pond in Yarmouth. The town was in the process of killing all the fish, draining the pond, refilling and restocking it. I think it's a wonder sometimes that we survive childhood. I waded around in the poisoned water for some time before anyone noticed me and coerced me out, eel in hand. That was the only eel I have ever seen, dead or alive, or somewhere in between.

Even my earliest dreams were of critters. I remember a dream I had when I was still sleeping in a crib. In the dream, monkeys were hanging from my crib bars, looking in at me. It was as if I were the helpless zoo animal and they were present to observe me. According to my recollection, this happened the same morning that my mother came in and found me dressed for the day. She spoke to me as a mother talks to a baby in a crib, not expecting an answer. "Who dressed you?" she asked, in exaggerated surprise, with bemusement on her face.

"Doody did," came my reply. I was referring to my teenage sister's friend, Judy Comstock. My mother was shocked and amazed at the quiet observations of a baby whose vocabulary, to her knowledge, did not extend much beyond "Mama". Peals of laughter followed and the story was repeated throughout the house, and for several years following. It may be that such a big deal was made over the fact that I actually answered her question, that the memory of the dream I awoke from that morning just kind of tagged along with the memory of when everyone was laughing at me. In any case, it's one of my first recollections.

In the only other dream I recall from a young age, my mother and I were walking in the woods and I saw a large snake slithering onto the branch of a tree over my head. The sight of it elicited excitement and glee.

* * *

One highlight of my childhood was when a nest with four baby robins fell out of a tree. One bird was dead, but I gathered the rest of the nearly featherless pink-looking creatures, put them back in the nest and brought them to my mother. She told me that the mother bird wouldn't want them after I had handled them, which happens to be a myth, but I'm sure she believed it at the time. I thought, "That's great! Now I can bring them up!"

In those days wildlife clinics didn't exist. I didn't understand that baby birds live on a diet of mostly insects and should be fed every ten minutes for fourteen hours a day. If not properly fed they have developmental problems that lead to premature death. I did the best I could with my limited knowledge. I put the robins in our basement and fed them a cereal mixture from an eyedropper. I think I later cut up earthworms for them. I won't elaborate on what happened to one of them, but suffice it to say that two survived. When they were full-size I let them go. One of them, whose leg I banded, would fly back to me from the wooded area in our backyard and land on my hand. It seemed almost too good to be true! I felt like Snow White.

* * *

Speaking of dreams come true, you can imagine my utter satisfaction when my husband Jesse and I found a house on a pond in a private setting with a big backyard and a plethora of wildlife. The pond was frequented by a blue heron. We saw a variety of waterfowl, including swans and cormorants. The realtor gave us a bird feeder that looked like a bird hotel, which we filled with sunflower seeds and cracked corn. Talk about critters! Each night we would see a big fat raccoon on top of it opening one of the roof flaps and helping himself to the contents. There were possums and skunks at night eating what dropped to the ground, and during the day there were mallards, quail, geese, and even two colorful wood ducks in the yard. The wood ducks were drawn here, I'm told, because there is a marsh area called Snow Pond that is partially on our property. We also are near to the power lines so we saw hawks aplenty, often perching on the utility poles and eyeing the large field that we call our backyard. There were red-tailed, sharp-shinned, and cooper's hawks, and swooping low around the marsh area were the harriers, or marsh hawks. All these visitors made for great viewing but there was a problem. We had created a feeding station, not only for the nocturnals and our feathered friends, but for the coyotes and foxes as well. At one time we counted twenty-one geese and three dozen ducks. We began finding the remains of ducks in

Bandy

the yard, but what finally cured us of wanting to keep the feeder up was when a rat began running out to it from under the deck, predictably, every five minutes. He never stayed more than a few seconds, perhaps sensing that he could be picked off by someone higher up in the food chain. Even my husband was tempted to bump him off. Needless to say, the feeder came down.

TWO

The Band

Although somewhat diminished, the wildlife sightings didn't stop when the feeder came down. We had made a few friends. One that stood out to me was a goose with a band around his right leg. With the help of binoculars I was able to decipher the numbers, "848-76258", and the words, "Bird Band Service, Laurel, MD", followed by a phone number. I jotted it all down and tucked it into a novelty cup on top of the refrigerator.

I enjoyed feeding and watching this goose and his mate as they came up from the pond to graze in our backyard. Male geese are generally larger than the females, and much more aggressive, so when they were together it was easy to tell the sexes apart. I observed the way the female would graze while the male stood guard for predators, then they'd switch off.

How they depended on each other! They came to trust us and I guessed they really liked cracked corn, because occasionally they would come up on the deck and look in the windows as if searching for the cracked corn distributors.

Spring turned to summer, summer to fall, and our friends were gone, but come late winter there were geese in the yard again. I got out my binoculars and read the band on one goose's ankle and jotted it down. I then compared it to the number in the cup on the refrigerator and it was the same goose as the previous year, only something was disturbingly different this year. His mate had been injured. She had a severe limp and would often stand on one foot and honk. The male would then imitate her behavior, as if to empathize with her.

I decided to report the banded bird's number to the Maryland bird band service. I was pleased that a goose came to this address, perhaps all the way from Maryland each year. In no time I received a "Certificate of Appreciation", not from Maryland, but to my surprise, it came all the way from Westboro, Massachusetts and was issued by the Division of Fisheries and Wildlife. It indicated that the goose was, in fact, a male. He was banded in Brewster on 7/12/95, and hatched in 1994 or earlier.

I placed a call to Mr. H. W. Heusmann who was named on the certificate as the man in charge of the bird banding operation and the ensuing conversation proved enlightening. He explained that the geese are banded for purposes of tracking. Those doing the banding and conducting the study have learned, among other things, that geese can live to be twenty years old. He also explained that many of our local geese do not fly south for the winter because they are the offspring of live decoys. "What's a 'live decoy'?" you might ask. It sounds like an oxymoron. I posed the question to Mr. Heusmann. He explained that prior to 1935 there was a common practice among waterfowl hunters of either purchasing baby geese or raising them from goslings for the express purpose of hunting. They would be tethered to a lead weight by a six foot cord with little cuffs around their legs. This almost inevitably led to injury and it was later ruled that the cuff had to be placed around the bird's neck instead. The hunter would hide behind a blind, and the tethered goose would fly back and forth in a limited way. Because geese are social birds, others would fly in when they saw and heard the decoy geese, thus, the hunter would get his prey. This was such a prevalent practice that the federal government limited each hunter to twenty-five live decoys, then outlawed them altogether in 1935 and ordered the release of thousands of captive geese. Now, almost seven decades later, generations of geese have not learned from their parents to fly south because their ancestors knew only captivity. Ironically, our year-round geese don't know where Canada is, nor do they know their way to the Carolinas.

The cold isn't really a problem for our geese—they're wearing goose down! What can become a problem for them, though, is getting food. If we have snow and a long spell of freezing temperatures it is actually possible for them to starve to death. They survive mostly on grasses and pond greens. I have discovered that they also really like cracked corn.

"Making Friends"—Bandy checking out the newcomer

THREE

Making Friends

During the winter of 2002 we had very little snow. My husband, before moving to Cape Cod, lived in New Hampshire, or "snow country", as we might call it here. If the weatherman predicts a three to five inch snowfall for the Cape, the grocery store parking lots are jamming while we all stock up on a week's worth of necessities, and school is likely to be canceled. Not so in New Hampshire. Snow is what they're used to, and unlike us, they can handle it.

Jesse loves the benefits of snow, whether cross-country skiing, winter camping or building snow forts and snowmen. I can recall nights of repeatedly waking up and checking the frigid temperatures on the weather channel while Jesse slept peacefully in a tent in the woods. It didn't seem fair. I had to get it through my head that while he was sleeping outdoors with an eight degree wind chill factor, it didn't bother him like it bothered me. And I was snug in a warm bed! Of course, he had all of the necessary accouterments to keep him warm and dry.

Before his days of computer absorption, little snow was a big disappointment to Jesse, but when that's all we got, he did his best with it and built a little snowman. I went to the back door after one particular miniscule snowfall to admire my husband's latest handiwork in the yard, and, to my surprise, my favorite goose was standing face to face with it as if trying to figure out this frosty newcomer. I found his curiosity and his seeming desire to communicate endearing, and I decided to name him. "Bandy", I mused. "Let's call him 'Bandy', after his band." He was so outgoing as if he wanted to be friends, not only with us, but with a snowman that was just his height.

"His girlfriend needs a name, too," I said.

"How about 'Bindy'?", Jesse suggested. We had only recently heard the name from Steve Irwin, the Crocodile Hunter. He and his wife had named their first baby Bindy. It went perfectly with Bandy, so from then on they were Bandy and Bindy.

Because of Bindy's limp and Bandy's band they were easily distinguishable from the other geese that made appearances in the yard. There were a few other mated pairs around and we would sometimes see them walking up and down our little street, which was for us an unusual and amusing sight. Geese mate for life, so they are often inseparable.

A fox was frequenting our yard at this time. We had witnessed many a squirrel becoming lunch—sometimes three a day. Although a gorgeous animal, this was what the fox was all about. He was a pretty predator, continuously on the prowl. I dreaded him coming when Bandy was in the backyard, but one day, it happened. At the first encounter, Bandy raised himself up, spread and flapped his wings and honked, moving toward the fox in an aggressive manner. The fox was intimidated and ran away. Good going Bandy! He held his own and I was quite proud of him.

The next encounter I witnessed didn't go as well. At first Bandy tried to make himself big and scary but this time the fox seemed persistent and Bandy decided to retreat and take flight. He put himself between the fox and Bindy, letting her go first to the pond, but before he managed to get himself off the ground the fox chomped on his behind, pulling out several feathers. Poor Bandy! He seemed to sit for hours in the middle of the pond, honking and mourning the loss of his tail feathers. Perhaps his pride hurt even more than his tail end. At one point, Bindy appeared to be ticked off that he seemed anchored to the middle of the pond. She stood on the shore, honking out her displeasure, then decided to come up alone for some cracked corn. For a mildly handicapped goose, she was pretty independent. Eventually, Bandy regained his confidence and joined her, and to my relief, the fox disappeared for a while.

Our geese grew pretty comfortable in the yard and all was well. Then one day someone new showed up. He was an extremely aggressive Canada goose with little white eyebrows that slanted upwards. This sinister-looking interloper would often chase Bandy and Bindy out of the yard. Terrorist that he was, he earned the name "Osama". His pregnant-looking mate was "Mama". We took to chasing Osama away any time we could, but we felt sorry for Mama. She was an absolute character who did something uncommon for a goose. Our house has a lower deck and a second floor deck and Mama would fly up to the second deck and sit on the rail. I surmised she thought she was a song bird. To our amazement, she even flew up higher to a small section of roof below the third floor windows and looked in. She did that more than once because she left her calling card behind as proof! One time our neighbor on the pond told me a goose would come and sit on their deck rail. "Oh, that's Mama," I said matter-of-factly. She certainly was one of a kind.

    I called Mr. Heusmann to ask about the aggressive goose and he informed me that the geese with white eyebrows are a subspecies. I pondered why this mean goose had to come and make Bandy's life miserable, but later in the story you will read how I actually came to appreciate him. Even a goose can change his attitude.

* * *

    Bandy and Bindy made it through the summer despite the harassment. This was "home" to them, I was their friend, and they knew it. As a matter of fact, it is quite likely that they were hatched on our pond and have lived here longer than we have. Geese tend to return to the place where they were hatched and Bandy's certificate indicated that he was banded in Brewster as a young goose. Griffith's pond is also the place where they do their molting, along with a dozen or so other geese. During the summer molt they lose their flight feathers and are usually confined to the pond. Of course, they can walk on land during this period, but they don't often choose to because without their flight defense they would be no match for predators in a showdown.

"Silly Goose"—Mama standing on deck rail

FOUR

Coyotes in the 'Hood

During the six years we've lived here we have seen several coyotes in our backyard. There's the large three-legged one who trots through seemingly unhampered by his amputation. It is amazing to me that a wild dog could endure such trauma, recover, run so well, and keep returning year after year—proof that an amputee can survive the wild. Perhaps he was the victim of an illegal leg-hold trap.

It is a common sound these days to hear a chorus of coyotes—something I never heard until I moved to this wooded area close to the power lines and abutting the Brewster Sportsman's club. There are about five ecozones that meet on our property. We are on a pond and our backyard is a large field that touches woods on two sides. We have the power lines, and we also have a wetland, or fresh water marsh, which is adjacent to Griffith's pond. Then there's the front yard, on a cul-de-sac, from which we have the flavor of a neighborhood.

It used to be that the high power lines were constructed to run parallel to communities, but now with so much development and the reaching of maximum buildout, we occasionally have power lines running through suburbia. Because the electric company needs access to the lines, you will notice rugged jeep trails that run along underneath them. These trails act as a route, or highway, if you will, for wild animals. The particular section of lines that passes through our backyard connects the Punkhorn Parklands and Nickerson State Park, which are about three miles apart. These are the two largest undeveloped wooded areas in Brewster. The Punkhorn consists of 900 plus acres that have been acquired by the town. It harbors a series of horseback riding trails, footpaths and a watershed protection area. The 2,000 acre state park is around three miles in diameter at its widest point. Both of these places are excellent havens for wildlife.

Coyotes and foxes are always on the move. They use footpaths and riding trails, and they use power lines wherever they're available. With the power lines crossing over our back lawn, it is no wonder that we are often treated to coyote songs. Sometimes their howling sounds like a shrill tremolo with intermittent yipping and yowling. On one occasion this performance sounded so close that my husband flipped on the back floodlight and there they were! A pack of coyotes was making its way across the backyard. Another night they were singing out dramatically on the side of our house at about the same time our neighbor's beautiful cat Emma disappeared. I later wondered if it was a victory song.

Although to us our cats are communicative little admirers, to coyotes they're just an easy, hearty meal. Coyotes are looking to survive like the rest of us—a good reason for us to keep our cats indoors, or our small dogs, for that matter.

My cat, Honey, spent his first four years as an outdoor cat. Though he nearly lost his right eye on one outdoor escapade, there was nothing he liked better than being free and able to hunt. As a matter of fact, when it came time to bring him in for the night he used to play a game with me. He would sit, calm and stationary, until I approached within grasping range, then he would bolt to another location and sit and stare at me like a taunting child. One night he repeated this mischievous prank about eight times. When it became clear that he was faster and trickier than I was, I finally gave up and left him outdoors for the night. It caused me to wonder if what I was being forced to put up with was retribution for all the things I'd inflicted on my mother as a teenager. Honey is no longer allowed outside. He is a prisoner of love.

Before marrying Jesse I spent several years living in upstairs apartments, which I purposely chose to discourage my cat from crying at the door. I figured a hall would be less of a temptation than the great outdoors. When we moved to Brewster he had panoramic views of the outdoors from the ground level. There were ten Anderson rollout windows and a glass slider for a back door. And I've already mentioned the critters. It was like IMAX Theater for kitty cats. All of the wonderful sights stirred up Honey's old yearnings to run free and be a part of what he could only behold from behind the glass. We were adamant about not letting him out with the coyotes in the neighborhood, though it took some discipline to resist his pleas. After a year or so of living in Brewster, he gave up crying for the outdoors. Our patience paid off. We allow him into the garage once we've settled in for the night. That gives him a door to cry at and a sense that he's getting his way. At least he won't fall prey to a coyote or try to compete with a moving vehicle. He also has the chance to catch an occasional mouse, or to corner a snake or a yellow spotted salamander, all of which he has done in our garage. He recently celebrated his fourteenth birthday, so indoor life must be agreeing with him.

One priceless sight we saw in our backyard was a coyote pup hunting. Success! After pouncing a few times he caught a small black wiggly critter, probably a mole or vole. And wouldn't you know, my husband captured it on video!

Thankfully, one thing I've never witnessed in the backyard is any confrontation between our geese and the neighborhood coyotes. Most of the coyote activity is after dark when the geese are hunkered down for the night. Our geese like to sleep on a large rock that is surrounded by water on the far side of the pond. They are pretty canny, and so far I only know of one of them being taken by a coyote. She was nesting at the time and trying to protect her eggs.

Occasionally, we spot a coyote during the day, such as the three-legged one. These daytime sightings are likely to be of transients attempting to avoid run-ins with the resident coyotes.

I have one final comment about living in such close proximity to the high power lines. When we first looked at the house, the sight of the power lines almost overpowered the beauty of the house and the natural setting. My brother-in-law offered the encouraging story of how his parents moved to a house under the high power lines, and in ten years, they were both dead. Of course, they were senior citizens when they moved there, but that seemed to be beside the point. The realtor told us that after a while we wouldn't even notice the power lines. I was skeptical, but as it turns out, the realtor was right. What we have enjoyed in our backyard: leaping, prancing deer, sometimes drinking at the pond or nibbling at the bushes, howling coyote packs; cute, fat little woodchucks sitting on their haunches as they grasp and munch clover, great blue herons fishing in the shallow water, then tilting their heads back to swallow their catch whole; I could go on and on. I could never have seen all of this beauty living in a development. As long as I have a choice, I will take the power lines and the wilderness experience any day!

FIVE

A Christmas Miracle

We had become accustomed to our geese leaving around the end of July when their flight feathers grew back, and they didn't return to our property until late winter, usually when there was some snow still on the ground. This year was no different. After they left I would sometimes hear geese flying overhead. I would look up and yearn for Bandy and realize just how much a goose had stolen my heart. Could my little backyard friend be in that curious and graceful "V" formation? Wherever he was, I was sure he'd be back.

The geese were gone, but our yard wasn't devoid of wildlife. Autumn seemed to bring out the fox. We would observe him on his relentless pursuit of squirrels. He would sometimes chase a squirrel up the stairs onto the second deck, from which the squirrel would then run down a support post to the first deck. Unlike the squirrel, the fox had to use the stairs. He'd turn and run down to the lower deck and the squirrel would climb the post up to the second deck again. Up and down, up and down. It was when a squirrel tried to escape and attempted a mad dash out towards the middle of the yard that he would inevitably lose the game.

I always had my camera handy and did get some pictures of the fox, but they were never up close and personal. How I wanted to get a great photo of that fox! Then his visits stopped.

It was early December and I told my husband that all I really wanted for Christmas was a good picture of the fox. Then I said one of those prayers that you almost feel silly praying as an adult, like, does God really care about this?

On the Saturday morning before Christmas I was downstairs cleaning, when suddenly something caught my eye outside the slider. I had thrown some sunflower seeds out on the concrete patio. They weren't birdseed, but rather, my snack food. I don't know what possessed me to throw them there, because I've never done that before or since. I was just getting rid of them because I'd had them too long. Well, there was the fox, right there on the other side of the glass! I sidled up to the slider, camera in hand, and began to snap pictures. He was only about four feet away from me, and kept looking up at me, but he wasn't intimidated. He was busy eating sunflower seeds for a full five minutes while I did my photo shoot! What a great Christmas gift! Don't tell me prayers don't get answered!

Just as mysteriously as the fox had presented himself at my door, he disappeared and was not spotted again for months.

"Christmas Gift"

SIX

Heartbreak

It was one cold, snowy day at the end of February 2003 when Jesse announced that he'd heard geese on the pond. It also happened to be a Saturday, our day off. I gathered some things to feed them and secured my goose call. After all, they would have a difficult time finding food with the pond mostly frozen and several inches of snow on the ground. Upon arriving at the shore's edge I didn't see them, so I blew the goose call. I was eager to know if it was Bandy and his friends that Jesse had heard. "Honk-a, honk-a", I blew. Suddenly from out of nowhere four geese came flying in my direction. As they came in for a landing I noticed one had a band. I was so excited! I was sure this was them. Then my heart sunk as I noticed that one of the four was missing a foot. "Look", I said to Jesse, who had just arrived,

"Bindy's leg finally came off. Poor thing!" The stump appeared still red on the end, as if it was a fresh wound. I figured her affliction, whatever it was, did its final dastardly deed. And there was Bandy, big as life, fighting the others to get the cracked corn I threw on the ice. They often pull each other's feathers when they compete for food. Bandy did his share of feather-pulling and got much of the food much of the time, or so it seemed. This may have contributed to the fact that he looked bigger than the rest of the geese. It was great to have them back.

Sunday morning we were off to church. When we arrived home my mother-in-law, Ginger, said something that hit me like a ton of bricks. "You know," she began, "I think that's our Bandy with the missing foot. He was up here today in the backyard and he was with Bindy, the goose that limps."

"No," I protested, "I know it's not. I saw Bandy pulling feathers. I know his personality, and he was the goose with the band."

"I think it's Bandy," she repeated softly, as if hoping not to hurt my feelings, yet making the point.

Well, that was that. I got my binoculars and went down to the pond. The geese came readily to meet me. I positioned myself to read the banded bird's number: "848-76...", so far so good. That was Bandy's number, alright. I strained to see the last three digits. "Come on, goose, *turn* so I can see the "258"! There it is: "848-76... *338*!" It wasn't Bandy! It was Bandy's best friend, one of the foursome that Bandy was a part of. That said it all. Sadly, Ginger was right. Something horrible had befallen my Number One goose. I knew now that it was Bandy, though his identifying band was gone with his right foot.

I walked up to the house, tears streaming down my face. When I broke the news to Jesse I burst into sobs.

"It's just a goose!" Jesse exclaimed.

"No, he's not 'just a goose', he's *my* goose!" I wept freely and began to go through a box of tissues.

"I think *you're* a silly goose!" my husband said. He didn't understand my affection for this favorite goose of mine. Why, of all the geese, did this have to happen to him? I couldn't control my crying and I ended up with a sinus headache.

"Oh, Bandy! I'm so sorry for you, my little friend!"

The next day when we returned home from work, the four geese came up to the back door for food. The snow was several inches deep. The air was crisp and cold, and darkness was already beginning to settle on the backyard scene. I turned the outside light on and tossed some corn to Bandy, Bindy, "338", as he had come to be called, and the goose I assumed to be his mate. I watched for a while to see how Bandy was managing in his newly altered state. The geese stood atop the hard crust that had developed over the snow and I saw Bandy moving his little stump back and forth as if trying to put a foot down that no longer existed. He leaned his weight to one side to keep his balance, but would sometimes lose it and land in the snow. This was apparently all very new to him, notwithstanding, he had the mindset of the lead goose that he had been, because he was still the one who told the others when it was time to finish up and go back to the pond. He did this by throwing his head in the air rhythmically and repeatedly, then doing the same while honking. The others began to turn towards the pond, take position, then they all took flight behind Bandy. "You are still the coolest goose, Bandy," I thought. "Nothing can take that from you."

The scene we witnessed that night was repeated several times over until the snow finally melted and the feeling of spring was in the air. When warmer weather arrived so did some of the other geese. Among them were Osama and Mama. Mama looked pregnant again, though up to this point we had never seen her with goslings.

Meanwhile, Bandy was coming up in the backyard alone. It seemed he would listen for our car to drive in over the long stone driveway, because no sooner did we get in the house, then we'd see this big bird flapping and hopping his way up the incline from the pond to the back door.

You couldn't really blame Bindy for leaving Bandy and taking up with "338". Yep. That's exactly what happened. She left Bandy for his best friend. She probably thought he could no longer be a good protector, and she was probably right, but geese mate for life and this may have hurt him more than losing his foot. I thought he must need company, so I took to sitting with him when he came up, and I'd watch for predators while he ate. During this time we bonded more than ever. I became certain that Bandy listened for my car, because my mother-in-law said that he wouldn't come up all day, but the moment we drove in, he'd start up the hill. It was just amazing.

"Who are you, Buddy?"

SEVEN

Birds of a Feather?

For a short while Bandy found another female friend. They would come up, graze, and sit together in the sun.

One day I looked out and saw who I thought was Osama coming to harass Bandy. I went out to chase him away when I momentarily got a better look at this stranger's face. It wasn't Osama. As a matter of fact, I wasn't sure it was a Canada goose! Certainly, the body was similar, but the legs were orange. It had a white face, a little black cap, and a colorful bill that was mostly orange with a tinge of pink and a black stripe up the center. Wow! It looked like a Canada with a mask on. I went back to the house for some cracked corn and my camera. I found this unusual visitor to be friendly and a taker for the corn and I was able to get several pictures of him. That is, until Bandy saw me feeding him and came furiously honking and chased him away! It was exciting while it lasted and I have the pictures as evidence that it really happened, but I was also happy that Bandy felt superior to someone.

One spring day I noticed Bandy sitting in the yard with another goose, only this time it wasn't a female. It was Osama, and they seemed to be getting along. This began happening on a regular basis, and, furthermore, Osama appeared to be Bandy's only friend. Where was Mama? We guessed she must be nesting somewhere. In any case, I decided I'd better start being nice to Osama. Reaching out to him was not an easy task, for the simple reason that I had traumatized him for so long by constantly chasing him away. Unfortunately, to this day, he sees me and runs. If I throw cracked corn to him he winces and ducks before he understands that I am giving him something. I'm so sorry, Osama! What caused you to change your attitude towards Bandy?

Around this time something delightful happened. One of the female geese had laid some eggs and, before long, there were two little yellow fuzz-balls running around the backyard with their parents. On the very day that they hatch they can run, swim, and find food for themselves, though their parents are right there guarding them tenaciously. By throwing them some corn I was able to lure them all very close for pictures. The goslings were only hours old. I watched as they laid on their bellies on the beach and stretched their little legs behind them, first one, then the other. They were absolutely adorable, like downy yellow chicks with big dark eyes. What a treat to have this addition to our backyard family and to be able to

Bandy

watch them grow. We called their parents Mother Goose and Father Goose. Father Goose, or "0958-79755", was only three years old himself and was hatched in Yarmouthport. There was one drawback to having "the family", as we came to call them, around. There is a strong pecking order among geese. If you are a single goose you are a nobody, or worse yet, you are suspect. If you have a mate, you are climbing the social ladder, and if your family is growing you can be downright oppressive. Pardon the expression, but Father Goose was a bona fide jerk to all of the other geese, while my number one goose fell into the "suspect" category. Bandy was so passive in the presence of this in-your-face new guy on the block that he preferred to simply practice avoidance. He began forfeiting coming up for corn and even chose staying as far away from the other geese as possible so long as Father Goose was around. Father Goose couldn't stand for any of the others to get any special treatment. It all belonged to him and his clutch. Moreover, I think even Jesse and I belonged to him and his family in his estimation. He would charge at all of the others with his neck stretched out and his head low, like some kind of hissing torpedo. I quickly tired of him and could only imagine that those cute little goslings were going to end up just like him.

In addition to being friendly with Osama, Bandy was sometimes spotted swimming with ducks. At other times he was all alone. He enjoyed hanging out at a place we call "goose point", directly across the pond from our beach. On occasion, "the family" would be out of sight and all I would have to do is appear on our beach. No matter if Bandy was all the way across the pond, he would make a beeline for me. I always rewarded him with corn or some great kind of bread from the natural food market, like sprout bread or grain and seed bread. I didn't make any noise so as not to tip off the family that I was handing out free victuals. I simply appeared, waved, and here would come my sharp-eyed friend. I found this amazing, but after a while Father Goose caught on. If he was around the bend where I couldn't see him from my beach and he couldn't see me, and Bandy started swimming my way from directly across the pond, suddenly Father Goose would appear out of nowhere and charge at Bandy. At first I thought it was coincidence, but then it happened over and over again. It seems there were jealous eyes trained on Bandy. Someone knew he was favored and took cues from him. I had to devise clever ways to treat him special.

At first I tried paddling out to him in the kayak. Situated on the other side of the pond to the right of goose point is a family campground and I hoped the other geese would mistake me for one of the campers we often see paddling around the pond in their canoes or flat-bottom aluminum boats. It worked for a while, but eventually I couldn't venture out without being chased by several geese.

Finally I devised an ingenious plan. When the geese came up in the backyard to graze I stationed my husband in the adirondack chair tossing small amounts of corn to them. I quickly drove to the neighboring road that led to the pond, only on the other side. To my dismay, three new houses had been constructed on the cul-de-sac since I had last traveled to the end of that road and it was now impossible to get to goose point without trespassing on private property! How could I reach Bandy? I summoned some chutzpah and made my way up one of the driveways where a family was cleaning their garage. "Hi, my name's Marcia." I proffered my hand. "I'm your neighbor from across the pond."

"I'm Becky," the lady of the house returned my gesture. I began to brief her about my goose as her family listened in. When I got to the part about him being picked on by the other geese I lost my composure. After all, he was my friend and I felt his pain. I wasn't making any conscious effort to elicit sympathy for him or for me, but this lady was certainly sympathetic. She assured me that I was doing a kind thing being concerned for him and she gave me a pass to cut through her yard any time I needed to get to him. Ah, what we won't do for a loved one! Pleased as punch that these were friendly and forgiving people, I proceeded to cut through Becky's well-groomed yard and down through the woods to goose point. There was Bandy, just where I had seen him through my binoculars from the other side of the pond. He met me eagerly as I offered him corn and he ate to his heart's content, while the other geese were none the wiser. Operation "sneak treat" was a success!

On at least one other occasion I cut through Becky's yard, after spotting Bandy standing on a spit of land between goose point and the campground. I pitied him standing so alone with his back to the pond. At the realization that he seemed depressed, I sat down with him and had a good cry. After feeding him some corn and speaking kindly to him, I stood and scanned the pond. There on the periphery was a swan. Desiring for Bandy to have some company, I waved several slices of bread in the air and lured him over. What was I thinking? I knew he got along fine with the geese, but being caught up in the moment, I forgot that

I was scared of him! I had been chased by this same swan and his mate before. He was huge. His neck was green with algae and he often had aquatic vegetation draped around it like a Hawaiian lei. He arrived at the shore and rose up out of the water, hissing loudly. My 120 pound frame felt suddenly feeble and a hasty retreat seemed like an intelligent strategy. I only hoped Bandy didn't find his presence as distasteful as I did, but I didn't stick around to find out.

"Baby-face"—One of the goslings born in our yard

EIGHT

Premonition

It was late June and the atmosphere on Griffith's Pond was short of ducky. Father Goose was well established as the pond bully and his goslings were swiftly approaching his stature. As if it were not inconvenient enough for the geese to have lost their flight feathers due to the natural molting process, Father Goose was on hand to pull out several more from every goose that happened to be minding his own business. They were all intimidated by him and tried to stay out of his way. Our shore's edge was littered with quills and down, and loud honking and tussles were the order of the day.

Bandy steered clear of it all. We had established a little meeting place that I directed him to, just over the property line of my neighbor on the pond, where there was a little inlet edged with dense vegetation for me to crouch in undetected. When the others were up grazing in someone else's yard I would silently appear on the shore, and wherever Bandy was he would make a beeline to our hideaway. I was pleased that he "got it". Bandy could swim under the leafy branches that overhung the water and the two of us were invisible. It was like a secluded pool where my friend was able to eat his favorite food in an undisturbed manner.

One night I had a vivid dream. It was of Bandy sitting across the pond on the edge of the woods with his back to the water. When I went to check on him he was visibly full of infection. I told the dream to my husband and added, "There's probably nothing to it, but rather, it's just a result of seeing him acting unlike the Bandy we know." I thought he had become withdrawn because of Father Goose, but he was also a little lethargic and was becoming harder to feed. One rainy day I didn't feel like subjecting myself to the elements so I didn't make the effort to walk the fifty or so yards to the pond. The very next day when I tried to get his attention he didn't come to me. I could see him at goose point, and there he remained.

"There's something wrong with Bandy," I told Jesse.

"Well, why don't you take the kayak out and check on him?" he suggested.

In just a few minutes I had crossed the pond to find my goose facing the shore and sitting in a puddle of blood. It took a moment to register because my first thought was that he was sitting on some red leaf litter. "No, it's not fall—there *are* no red leaves. My friend is in trouble," I ruminated, with a twinge of anguish.

Bandy

On my way back to the other side a conversation I'd had with Mr. Heusmann from the Division of Fisheries and Wildlife flashed through my mind. I had called him in late winter when Bandy had returned, minus his foot. I sought this man's expert advice on whether or not I should bring him to a wildlife rehabilitation center for treatment. Mr. Heusmann suggested that the goose had already suffered physical trauma and to capture him and put him in captivity would inflict emotional trauma on his already jangled psyche. He said the loss of his foot would probably shorten his life span, but he would most likely be happier to be left to live it in the wild without any human intervention. He also said that if I brought him for treatment they would either euthanize him or he would have to live the rest of his life in captivity. I had related the conversation to Jesse and to my mother-in-law Ginger, and they wholeheartedly agreed. But this was different, for sure. Bandy needed intervention this time. How could I convince my family? I hashed it all over in my mind, and when I got back to the house I first called my sister. She believes in prayer and animals' needs are every bit as important to her as peoples' needs. "Sheila, could you pray for Bandy?" I asked through my sobs, and I explained the circumstances.

"I already prayed for Bandy. Around three o' clock he came to my mind and I felt as though he was in some kind of trouble, so I prayed for him."

This was phenomenal, and very reassuring. Could it be that God was aware of his situation and would look out for him? Isn't the Sovereign Ruler of the Universe too lofty to concern Himself with a goose? Sheila didn't think so, and I guess I didn't either, or

I would not have asked her to pray.

Next, I called Wild Care, though it was almost two hours past closing time. After listening to my emotional blathering to an answering machine about my goose and blood, a gentle-voiced woman picked up the phone. She first tried to decipher if this was a pet goose or a wild goose. "Well, he's both, sort of."

She said if he was a pet, a regular vet is what I should seek. "Oh, he's definitely a wild Canada goose, but he was banded before he lost his foot and his band, and he's kind of tame. He's in some pretty bad trouble," I said in a voice that was cracking like a goose.

"Bring him in," she said.

I found Jesse and told him of Bandy's fate. His immediate reaction was to jump in the kayak and go see for himself. In the meantime I gathered some expendable towels and a large box, only to be met several minutes later by Jesse telling me there was no need to rush to Wild Care. He had checked out Bandy and thought that the blood was probably due to a scuffle with Father Goose or one of the others. "They just pulled out a couple of his feathers. See, I took a picture of the wound in back of his left leg." Jesse held up the tiny image on his digital camera for my viewing. "You should know he'll be okay. Look how he recovered from losing a foot. He has amazing powers of recovery, and just think, if we tried to bag him, he'd never trust us again."

This was so hard. My better judgment told me that he needed help, but now I had not only my husband, but also my mother-in-law advising me not to touch him. "You know what Mr. Heusmann said," they admonished.

Certain that I could not single-handedly capture and

transport a large, struggling goose, and feeling that any mishap would meet with an, "I told you so," I gave up the fight and prayed for him instead. Somehow that dream I'd had that Bandy was infected never once occurred to me. I guess I was too distracted by the situation at hand to recall it. I was resigned to hope that he could recover on his own.

Jesse offered to take me over in the rowboat for another look, as the kayak was suitable for only one person. While I was checking out the wound and source of the blood, Jesse decided to skulk around to see if there were any signs that an animal had attacked Bandy. He used to teach animal tracking at summer camps and can aptly identify things like tracks and scat, plus he was looking for signs of a struggle.

"Oh, no! This is awful!" I heard my husband exclaim from twenty feet away.

"What? What is it?"

I turned to see him picking up the carcass of a goose from the underbrush. All that was left was the ribcage and the skeletal wings with a few long feathers jutting out from each wing. I stood gazing for a solemn moment. "Mama," I opined. "That explains why there's no more goose sitting on the railings."

It also explained why Osama went from terrorist to outcast and became Bandy's best friend—sort of an alliance formed out of misfortune. Mama had been nesting and apparently goose point was her roosting ground. When approached by a coyote, a nesting female will lay herself flat over her eggs in absolute stillness, in hopes that the coyote won't see her. Mama's instinctive negotiations proved fatal.

Jesse and I boarded the rowboat accompanied by Mama's

remains—a solemn reminder that even in a tranquil setting like Griffith's pond, danger lurks about, and none is impervious to its intentions. Jesse wanted to include Mama, or what was left of her, in a documentary he was making for local public television about the lives of geese, including their potential fate. It was an unsettling day, to say the least.

NINE

A Friend in Need

The next day when we returned home from work my mind was on Bandy. Not really being the sporty type due to allergies and an occasional low back ache, I convinced Jesse to kayak over to goose point and check on him. Paddling around the pond in the past couple of weeks was beginning to take its toll on my back.

"He looks okay," Jesse said haltingly. "His leg looks a little hooked up on his body."

"What do you mean?" I decided to go over there the easier way, via Becky's yard, and check out the situation. I didn't see Bandy in his regular spot so I sought an alternate path to the water. It wasn't as if you could walk down to the water, then along the shore, because the water comes right up to the bushes in that area. I made my way down a trail that was grown over with brambles and underbrush, snapping and stomping small branches as I fought my way through the tangle. Due to the fact that Massachusetts is a tick-infested state, and Brewster is one of the deer tick capitals of Cape Cod, visions of deer ticks were dancing in my head. This, especially since my sister has been disabled from Lyme Disease. As I approached the water I saw Bandy right before me, sitting in the woods. This was highly unusual. I put some corn down and he took a few nibbles, then mustered the energy to turn away slightly. This was disastrous. He seemed barely able to move and he was vulnerable to coyotes if he stayed in the woods. He was sitting just feet from the spot where we'd found Mama. It was now seven o' clock and I knew nobody would be at Wild Care. Conflicted by Mr. Huesmann's advice to leave Bandy in the wild, and aware that Bandy was a wild animal who was adverse to human handling, I didn't know what to do. I was torn. I also didn't have any help up to this point, because I was the only one now convinced that he needed Wild Care. Soon the sun would go down on Cape Cod, but I hoped not on my goose.

The next morning Jesse, who is the early bird of the two of us, kayaked over to goose point before work to make sure Bandy had survived the night. Bandy was in the water now and Jesse thought he'd be okay for the day, but we determined taking him to Wild Care would be our first order of business when we got home.

The hours of the day could not pass quickly enough. As soon as we were through with work we parked on the cul-de-sac and cut through Becky's yard, racing to the spot where I'd last seen

Bandy

Bandy. He wasn't there. A quick scrutiny of the surrounding areas turned up a helpless goose, unable to swim and bobbing about in the water. His only whole leg was hooked way up on his torso. He was trying frantically to paddle with his stump to absolutely no avail. As I looked on, I was silently chastising myself for not acting sooner to help him. Jesse agreed to capture him for me regardless of anyone's sage advise, because it was obviously do or die.

We drove home and I placed a quick and desperate call to Wild Care as Jesse collected the gear we'd need for the rescue effort. The same young woman answered the phone and she told me to bring my goose on in.

Still unable to fly due to molting season, and impotent to swim away from us, Bandy was easy to catch, but not so easy to hang on to. Jesse threw a towel around a very frightened bird, then carried him, both of them struggling, to the open box waiting at the top of the hill. We loaded him in, taped the top, and prayed that he wouldn't hate us for this, then slid the box into the back of the station wagon and drove the mile or so to Wild Care. Lela, a pretty blonde girl who looked too young to be the director of the facility, greeted us in the entry way, then Jesse carried the bulky box to its resting place in the treatment area. He gave some words of explanation about Bandy's condition before leaving, then I tried as best I could to express that this goose was very important to me and I would be checking on his progress.

The next day I called to see how he was and whoever answered the phone had no information to offer. A little later on I just happened to be passing by, so I stopped in.

"Hi," I said to Lela. "I was just wondering if you've figured out what happened to my goose."

"We don't know what happened to him yet."

"Are you giving him antibiotics? He must have an infection, right?"

"Yes, we're treating him with antibiotics, but I hope you understand that we may have to euthanize him if he can't make it in the wild." She spoke hesitantly as if there was something she *wasn't* saying.

I tried to keep a stiff upper lip as I numbly mouthed the words, "Yes, I understand that if you can't fix his problem you'll have no choice but to put him to sleep." At the very thought of transporting him to his death, I couldn't hold back the emotion and tears began spilling down my cheeks. I thought of Mr. Heusmann's words: death or captivity. I apologized for the waterworks and said that I'd wait for her word.

That night around seven o' clock Lela called. "I wanted to say, you have a *really* neat goose."

"She likes him!" I thought. My heart was suddenly light as I listened with hope and interest.

"His problem is that he apparently got fishing line tied around his leg and it was so swollen that his circulation was being cut off *to the bone*," she said, emphasizing the last three words. The line was no longer there. Lela guessed that the puddle of blood was possibly from the swelling letting go and actually bursting his flesh and that perhaps the line had snapped from the pressure of the swelling. "We'll see what we can do for him. A vet will look at him on Tuesday, then we'll decide whether or not we can treat him."

Apparently Bandy had gotten entangled at least a couple of weeks prior to our finding him in his helpless state. The monofilament fishing line has a tendency to shrink. Add to that the fact that Bandy's leg was swollen out of proportion, and it's easy to understand why his circulation was completely cut off.

Lela and I conversed a little more, I thanked her for keeping me posted and hung up the phone. All at once it came back to me—the dream I'd had just two weeks before, and how accurately it had played out. I reminded Jesse of it, as he had forgotten, too. Although the dream didn't serve to ward off any trouble (since I remembered it way too late), it did cause me to know, if I never knew it before, that this goose and I were somehow inexplicably linked.

On Tuesday I got a most anticipated call. Lela said they decided to treat him.

"Up a Tree"—Jesse used to dress in this garb and sit in a tree stand to quietly observe the wildlife—that is, until a thief made off with the stand! In case you're wondering how this close-up was taken high up in a tree stand, my husband has long arms.

TEN

A Friend, Indeed

Although Jesse had seemed reluctant at first to bring Bandy for treatment, he really had a big heart for critters. There was the time we stopped to rescue a cat lying in the road. The people in the SUV in front of us drove right over it, being careful to straddle it, but they didn't stop. It was dazed and its eye was rimmed with blood. We didn't have a towel or anything to wrap it in, so Jesse scooped it up in his arms and was carrying it around like a little Raggedy Ann doll from house to house, looking for the owner. As he walked into one yard a dog lunged at him from the bushes. The cat flipped out of his arms and began running in circles, clearly affected by being smacked in the head. In the meantime, I had the job of first finding a place to park our Subaru Outback, then of frantically chasing away the dog. Jesse again cradled the cat and together we resumed the search for its owner. Nobody answered the four or five doors we knocked on. Finally we approached a live person in a car, leaving a driveway. We pleaded with him for any information that could lead us to the cat's owner and he directed us across the street. We crossed the busy main road and followed a long dirt driveway to a small house on the edge of the woods. I knocked for a good five minutes and we were about to give up, when finally the door opened and revealed a drowsy looking man. "I hope we're not disturbing you," I said, while thinking, "I know we just woke you up."

"I was asleep because I work nights, but that's okay. What's up?"

Jesse emerged from the shadows, holding the cat. "Is this your cat?" he asked. The man stepped out of the house to take a better look. "It was apparently hit by a car. We found it lying in the eastbound lane of Route 6A," Jesse explained.

"Yes, it's one that I feed, but I'm amazed you're holding it. It's a feral cat."

At the realization that this was no pussycat that my husband was hugging to his breast, fear seized my heart. Jesse was from New York City and I found out later that he had never heard of a feral cat, so the warning didn't ring any bells with him. Just then, the previously dazed cat awoke from his stupor, and, like a missile with claws, he launched himself at his feeder's face. In a split second there was a piece of flesh hanging from the man's nose, blood was gushing everywhere and the cat disappeared into the woods.

"Oh, I'm so sorry!" I exclaimed. The man, with bleeding

nose and watering eyes, thanked us for saving the cat's life, then hurried in to care for his wound. Jesse and I couldn't help but marvel at the miracle of being, ourselves, unharmed while carrying around a feral cat for fifteen minutes.

As we were leaving the property, I noticed an old vehicle out front with a "for sale" sign on it. I jotted down the phone number with the idea of checking on the welfare of both cat and man. When I called three weeks later, the man informed me that the cat, amazingly, was fine. He said he had once brought a feral cat to the vet and the bill was a thousand dollars. That particular cat was now tame and living in his house and was the mother of the cat we saved. He again told us how grateful he was for our efforts.

Injured feral cats were not the only thing Jesse had a motivating compassion for. One spring day while we were cleaning the Burr's house, a box turtle wandered into their garage in an apparent attempt to mate with a boot wipe that was in the shape of a turtle. Just then, old Walter Burr backed his car out of the garage. Unaware of the turtle, he ran over its front leg. Jesse stepped out to empty some trash and found the turtle near the boot wipe with its leg barely attached. There were no second thoughts about it—the turtle took precedence over the job. He left me to finish alone while he drove the ten miles to Wild Care.

It may well have been Jesse's desire to help the helpless that got him involved in my cleaning business. I had a partner who one day decided to temporarily relocate to Florida. Jesse was licensed and employed cutting hair, and aspired to one day buy Poppy's Barbershop, but when he saw me up the creek without a paddle, he came to my rescue. That was the end of his profession in hair. He wasn't crazy about cleaning, and never really intended to continue pushing vacuums and mops, but he found that mindless work was great for pursuing college degrees. At work he wore large orange earmuffs—the kind worn by landscapers—to block out the noise of the vacuum. One day he thought, "I may as well be listening to something instead of just blocking out noise," so he began wearing his walkman and tucking ear buds inside the muffs. In this manner he could study tapes relative to his college subjects. Life was good again for him, and more so for me.

* * *

Though Jesse had a rescuing heart, he hadn't felt settled about bringing Bandy for treatment prior to our actual decision to go ahead with the rescue effort. He was hoping the goose could recover on his own. Between Mr. Heusmann's advice to let Bandy be, and the fact that wild geese are so frightened by humans, the prospect of capturing him almost seemed unkind. And unlike turtles that are seemingly nonchalant about a ride in an automobile, we had read that a frightened goose could injure himself in transport out of sheer terror.

Though Bandy's condition was dire, I was hopeful that we'd gotten to him in time and I was also encouraged by Lela's interest. I sensed she would do the very best for him that could possibly be done.

I went to the pond daily in Bandy's absence and visited the other geese, wondering if they noticed that goose point was devoid of the loner. Did anyone miss him? Maybe they thought he went the way of Mama. Bindy was still an item with 338. Father Goose continued to dominate the pond. Osama was as skittish as ever in my presence. The goslings were still getting aquainted with their surroundings. I watched the pair as they played with a buoy near Jesse's makeshift dock. They would pull on the rope and peck at and turn the red cylindrical bobber with their bills, like children sharing a new toy. They were clearly young 'uns, though by now they were almost the same size as their parents. Besides being playful, they emitted an almost constant peeping sound that gave them away. They didn't have their honk yet. As I observed all of the activity on the pond, I decided I was probably the only one there missing Bandy. And did I ever.

On Monday I called Wild Care and left a message informing them that if for any reason they decided they couldn't treat him, I would pick him up and take him to a regular vet. I couldn't really afford it, but he was like a pet to me and I didn't want to lose him. The following day was when Lela called to say they decided to treat him. On Wednesday I stopped in so I could have a face to face with Lela. She told me the veterinarian had come in to work with Bandy. Though his appetite was good, they were giving him vitamins and trying to build him up because of his emaciated appearance when he arrived there. Over the summer I had watched him go from a big, healthy looking goose to a scrawny, scruffy one.

I also had some concerns that he might have lice because before we rescued him he seemed so itchy all the time. With no right foot he was unable to scratch his neck on the right side.

He had to do creative things like lay his head and neck across his back and rub like crazy to get relief, which even then seemed elusive. I so wanted to scratch his neck for him, but I didn't want to invade his space. Once I saw him bend his neck way over to the left, stick his head upside down in the water, and scratch the right side of his neck with his left foot. I told Lela about my concerns. After examining him, she said he had no external parasites, but she treated him for internal parasites in case they were the culprit responsible for his frailty. She assured me that he was being well cared for and that they would keep doing blood work to monitor the infection and his overall health.

Everyone who worked at Wild Care was well aquainted with Bandy because he spent most of his time in the bathtub. There was no shower curtain for the tub so anyone who had to use the facility had to do so with a goose looking at them. I guess that took some getting used to, but they all got to know him in an intimate setting. Whether or not Bandy thought the new setup stunk, I can't tell you. Perhaps he was left to ponder what it is that people don't like about geese, who are at least vegetarian, if you get my "drift".

I was feeling overall pretty optimistic about Bandy's recovery, until one day I stopped in again to check on his progress. Lela wasn't there so I posed my usual questions to a young woman in blue scrubs.

"He's doing okay, but you understand that we may have to euthanize him if he's not viable to live in the wild, right?"

"Why are they telling me this?" I wondered with incredulity. Had he taken a turn for the worse? I choked up as I tried to gain some clarity on his condition. "I'm sorry about my lack of composure. It's just that we've been friends for five years. We've spent a lot of time together."

My blubbering met with some surprised looks and I thought surely they must find it curious that I was acting this way over a wild Canada goose. Who could understand, after all, that I'm friends with a goose? Why should they even believe me? My final sentence seemed to end abruptly as it met with silence. I hung my head in sadness and mild embarrassment and quietly slipped out the door.

A few days passed without a word. I didn't want to hound or bother anyone by calling every day about a wild animal. I had to learn a lesson of trust. He was in the hands of experts. Then one day I came home from work to a message from Lela on My answering machine. I hurriedly returned her call, eager for a good word, and a good word I got.

"You have a great goose," she reiterated. "He's a *good little man.*"

Most people can relate to the companionship of a dog or cat, but Lela had once owned a Chinese goose and she could understand a human/waterfowl relationship. I felt I was communicating with a like-minded person who perceived the depth of soul that even a goose could possess. She went on to tell me of Bandy's progress, explaining that it would take time for him to regain the use of his left leg, but that they would work with him for as long as was required.

Apparently the good folks at Wild Care had been conflicted about whether or not to spare Bandy's life. They are required to euthanize rather than amputate, but Bandy arrived at the facility as an amputee, and his injury had nothing to do with the amputated leg. Still, they were uncertain about what measures to take, caught between gray area federal stipulations on the one side, and my emotional outbursts on the other. It seemed to have been when I asked for him back so I could bring him to a regular vet, that they made their decision to treat him. I was just relieved and thankful that Lela had come to show mercy on my little friend. She saw something in him that tugged at her heartstrings, too. To Bandy and me, she was a friend, indeed.

ELEVEN

There's No Place Like Home

It had been nearly a month since we'd brought Bandy in for treatment and I was beginning to get a little nervous that the rest of the geese were going to fly away without him. It was their custom to leave when their flight feathers grew back, and the goslings were already being escorted out for flight lessons so I knew the time was drawing near. I was afraid that if Bandy returned to an empty pond he would feel dejected. I also had concerns about the prospect of him coming home to the pond around the time when the geese were due to leave for the season, because I didn't want him to fly off to where I couldn't monitor his recovery. Then one Monday afternoon I received a phone call. It was Lela informing me that Bandy was good to go and we could pick him up anytime.

With excitement and anticipation, we gathered up the necessary gear and Jesse and I took to the road. When we arrived at Wild Care and checked in we were greeted with a sight I will never forget. It was Lela carrying Bandy enshrouded in a towel, with his head hanging down as far as it could hang, limp with the defeat of being restrained in human grasp. He looked so sad!

We loaded him into the box and headed for home. Once in the driveway, we opened the tailgate and gently placed the box on a boogie board, which is a styrofoam device with a draw cord used to surf the waves. This way we could easily glide the box down the slope to the pond. Jesse sat in the adirondack chair which he had placed down by the water. I opened the box lid and a skinny little neck and head poked up over the side. As Bandy looked out over Griffith's Pond, he seemed to revive at the recognition of his surroundings. I helped him out of the box. He quivered with delight, flapped his wings and made his way into the water. He was so excited he sounded two victory honks, then began paddling with vigor and dunking himself in the water. His antics and image defined a happy goose. From watching him that day, I don't think he ever thought he would see Griffith's Pond again. In no time he was out in the middle of the pond and it was evident that his newly healed leg was working just fine. Wildcare had done swimmingly!

The other geese happened to be out testing their flight apparatus when Bandy came home, but they soon joined him. I was happy to see that they were all together and that they all came to get corn without much quibbling, providing Father Goose wasn't there. He was away more than the others because of his offspring, who were probably getting a grand tour of all the fertile feeding grounds and waterways. The rest of the geese were back and forth to and from some other location, but Bandy stayed put on the pond. The question of whether he'd be a part of the gang when it came time to leave for the season nagged me. I was torn between not wanting him to feel isolated, yet wanting him to stay so I could fatten him up and take care of him. I think I experienced what some parents go through when they have a child with a condition that sets him apart.

The following Saturday morning I was watching Bandy all alone in the middle of the pond through my binoculars when I heard the geese flying in. They came, in formation, right over his head, then dropped to the water. As they did, he again emoted two honks. He put all of his body language into those honks and he seemed to be clearly saying, "I want to fly with you guys. I *so* want to fly with you! Please don't leave without me." The sight was touching and tore at my heart. Was he too weak to fly? Lela had deduced that he was depressed towards the end of his stay at the facility because his appetite had dropped off. It could not have been due to anything physical because he was all healed up and his blood work was good.

One week after Bandy was returned to us I went to the water's edge with some corn. All of the geese, including Bandy, came to enjoy it and I remember saying to Bandy, "You look beautiful!" He looked as if he had gained a pound or two in a week. He was filled out and he was one of the gang. I couldn't have hoped for better.

The following day we checked in at home between jobs and saw Bandy and all of the geese together. When we returned home two hours later all of the geese were gone. I stood at the water's edge and blew the goose call. No Bandy. I asked Jesse to paddle around the pond and check for anything amiss. A perusal of the entire perimeter of the pond turned up nothing. Bandy was gone. How could this happen? I hadn't even seen him fly yet. He had only been on the pond eight days. I didn't know whether to be happy or disappointed. In any case, I was a bit taken aback.

That evening we went to the town library, then to watch the sun set over the bay. Jesse brought his digital camera and began snapping pictures of the sunset when we noticed some little black specs out about a half mile. It looked like geese, so Jesse photographed them and brought the picture back to the computer where he was able to enlarge it and pan back and forth. They most certainly were geese—21 of them. "Look," my husband said, "even this group has a straggler." There was one goose alone on the outskirts of the group. To this day, I think it was Bandy.

TWELVE

Empty Nest Syndrome

Nearly a month went by and there was nary a visitor on the pond but for the great blue heron, some occasional ducks, and a male kingfisher sitting on the piling of our neighbor's timeworn dock.

I stopped in at Wild Care to chat with Lela and she asked me the inevitable question. "How's Bandy?"

"I don't know. He left the pond after only eight days."

Lela's eyes became wide with concern. Following a pregnant pause she asked, "How do you know a coyote didn't get him?"

"Because at 2:30 he and all of the geese were there, then when I checked at 4:30 they were *all* gone. They left together. There were no signs of a struggle anywhere around the pond, and besides, I have confidence in him. I'm ninety-nine percent sure he's fine."

I have to admit, I left there with my confidence a little shaken for no other reason than that the animal expert seemed so distracted by the news. On my way home I stopped at Ferretti's, the local family-owned market. While standing in line to make my purchase I noticed Mark, my next door neighbor, in front of me. After exchanging pleasantries, Mark divulged that he was experiencing a little empty nest syndrome. His kids had just returned to school after a fun summer during which they had basically done everything together. He thought it was neat that, though they are approaching their teens, they had all gone to movies together, spent a lot of time at the beach together, and done various other activities as a family. Mark had always seemed like an ideal dad to me. After all, he was owner of the Village Toy Store. What better business could a father be in?

"I'm experiencing an empty nest syndrome of my own," I confided. I went on to explain about my goose's plight and how since he left, the pond that we share with our neighbors seemed so empty.

Mark's girlfriend, Melissa, like myself, has a heart for animals. One time after Bandy had come back missing his foot she showed up at my door carrying a towel. She asked if I had any objections to her capturing the one-footed goose that she'd noticed in our backyard and bringing him to Wild Care. She thought his wound was fresh, but actually by then it had healed over somewhat. I assured her he was going to be okay and that when it first happened we were advised by Mr. Heusmann not to bring him. I appreciated her concern and she seemed consoled about his state.

Bandy

* * *

With the passage of time I couldn't help but wonder what happened to Bandy and it was really getting to me. I wished I could've seen him fly just *once*. I was given to little emotional upsets at unwelcome times. One Thursday I was changing a bed at a house I was cleaning, all the while thinking about how much I missed Bandy. The tears began to flow. Then I said a prayer:
"God, I know that you know where Bandy is. If he's still in the area, could you please show me where he is?"

The fact is, I hadn't seen *any* geese, *anywhere* in Brewster besides in our yard and the ones we'd seen on the bay the evening of our geese's departure. None of Brewster's golf courses can be viewed from the street and even the schoolyards are tucked out of sight.

The following Monday I had some business at Wild Care. We had released a banded Canada goose to our pond a couple of weeks earlier that had been treated at the facility. This goose was in good health and only stuck around for two days. I reported the goose's band number to the bird band service in Maryland and had obtained a certificate on it, a copy of which I was bringing to Lela.

"Here's that certificate you requested."

"Thanks. Oh, you'll never guess who I saw last Friday!" The look on Lela's face gave it away.

THIRTEEN

Goose Abuse!

"Bandy! You saw Bandy!"
Lela's smile broadened. "Yes, I saw Bandy. You won't like this part, but a woman called to report some goose abuse at Stoney Brook Elementary School."

"Not *Bandy!*"

"No, it was another goose. A female, I think. A boy ran his bike into a flock of geese and struck one of them. When I arrived the woman who reported it was on the scene and pointed to the victim."

"I think it was that one over there," she said, as she singled out Bandy.

Lela looked long and hard and responded, "No, I know that goose. He only *had* one foot and he otherwise doesn't appear to be injured." Then she noticed a goose limping, but as she tried to approach it they all flew away, with Bandy straggling behind.

My heart was filled with gratitude that my prayer was heard. At least someone had seen him and it gave me assurance that he really did make it, though I hadn't seen him for two months. Coincidence, you call it? I don't know, but it seems it's when I pray that these "coincidences" happen.

Two days later, and with the knowledge that Bandy was still in the area, I posed a question to Jesse: "Where would a Brewster goose be?"

"At the nearest golf course."

The fact is, I had a nagging concern that the limping goose might be Bindy, because she limped anyway and would be more vulnerable than the average goose. I was outraged that a child could wittingly hurt a goose, never mind an already handicapped goose like Bandy or Bindy. These were obviously our backyard geese that were accosted. My sweet, unassuming little friends. I even went to the playground to try and find out who did it. A small boy gave me the information. He said the boy had bragged about it in the lunchroom. With tears, I asked the informant to pass along a message to this misguided child. "Could you please tell him for me that these geese are like pets. They have *names*. I'm even writing a book about the one-footed goose and all I can say is, it had better not have been him that was hit."

I think my plea, complete with tears, made an impression on him and he promised to pass it on to the perpetrator.

FOURTEEN

Where Do You Wander?

Troubled by thoughts of who may have been hurt and how badly, I decided to go looking for our geese. Jesse and I drove to the nearest golf course, which happened to be part of a private condominium complex. It was guarded by men in booths at both entrances of the nearly two mile stretch between Route 6A and Route 137, with the golf course running nearly the entire length of the main throughway. We were presented with a formidable task: the prospect of trespassing to search for other trespassers at an exclusive place like Ocean Edge. How could we possibly gain entrance?

Jesse pulled up to the booth on the south end. "We volunteer for Wild Care," he explained to the security guard. It wasn't entirely untrue, since we had recently done a couple of goose releases. "We're trying to track a goose that's been injured and we don't know how badly. We thought it might be here."

It worked. The security guard let us in. As we drove slowly along we tried to peer between and beyond the condos over the sprawling green. The seemingly endless fairway disappeared behind buildings and trees in places, and stretched beyond our view in others. This was truly a daunting mission. In several minutes we were approaching the manned booth at the other end. So much for finding geese.

"Seen any geese around here?" Jesse asked.

"There are no geese on this golf course," came the guard's reply. Jesse gave him the same explanation for our presence that he had given the man at the other end. After a brief pause the second guard relented, "They like Blueberry Pond here on the premises. I hear them fly right overhead in the morning going that way." He pointed in the direction of the elementary school. "Then in the afternoon they fly back to the pond."

"Is it accessible?" I asked.

"Not by car. You can park behind the Reef Cafe and walk that way and down through the woods if you would like." He indicated the general direction of the pond.

Though I'm sure it wasn't the direction-giver's fault, how to approach the pond wasn't entirely clear to us, which provoked Jesse to say, "I'm not into this." He passed the cafe's parking lot and drove straight out to 6A, then proceeded to drive home. I wasn't satisfied. Where there's a will, there's a way, and I was willing to search it out. I dropped my husband off at home, turned around and went back to Ocean Edge. It was approaching six o' clock in the evening and I wasn't sure I wanted to go traipsing around in the woods at dusk on unfamiliar territory, but the presence of a guard nearby offered a small sense of security. Besides, I didn't want to spend a third night worrying about who might've gotten hurt. The prospect of seeing my bird was all the impetus I really needed to proceed with my hunt.

With a prayer, I made my way to the small lot behind the cafe and parked. I began my trek down the narrow paved path which I guessed to be a roadway for golf carts. It ran between the fairway and the wooded area that sheltered the pond. I glanced over at the green on my right and stopped dead in my tracks. My jaw must have dropped several inches, because what I saw looked surreal. Being totally unfamiliar with the pastime of golf, aside from the mini sort, I was taken aback by the grass, which looked like it was from another planet, especially around the holes. But that's not what shocked me. It was the thirty or so geese I saw *on* the green that I couldn't believe. Of all the places I could have entered this huge golf course, there they were on the very first stretch I encountered. "There are no geese on this golf course," rang back in my head. Maybe he was trying to protect the reputation of the fairway. Like a slow motion sequence in a movie I began to walk on this otherworldly grass towards the geese. My eyes darted to and fro as I scoped out their legs, in search of one missing a foot. Might this be the moment that I actually see Bandy?

Once among them I saw some familiar faces. First I recognized "the family". The five month old goslings, though visually indistinguishable from their parents, were still peeping. Father Goose ran towards me to see what I had to offer him. There was Bindy with her limp, which seemed no more severe than when I had last seen her. She apparently wasn't the victim at the elementary school. She was with "848-76338", better known as "338", who sported a recognizable little point on the back of his head that was reminiscent of a bicycle helmet. There was shy Osama with the eyebrows, hanging out with Bindy and 338. The only one of my familiar geese that I didn't see was Bandy. I continued walking among them until every last seated goose got up and I was able to check their feet.

Troubled and determined, I parted company with the geese and quickened my steps towards the pond. With goose call in hand, I followed the winding path through the woods to the water. "Honk-a, honk-a," I blew again and again. There was not a goose to be found on the pond. Now I was beginning to wonder if it was Bandy who'd been injured on the playground. With my allergies to mold and dampness, and my fraidy cat nature, no other scenario I can imagine could send me wending my way down a lengthy path through the woods at dusk.

With waning confidence that I'd ever see my goose again, I plodded up the hill from the pond, surfaced from the woods, and stood for a moment in time gazing sadly at thirty geese. Without warning and breaking my stare, came the steady flap, flap, flap of a huge pair of wings. There in the distance was a bird flying towards me at eye level, gliding over the green landscape. "Bandy!" I shouted. No doubt, it had to be him. He approached, let down his lopsided landing gear and dropped practically at my feet. "Bandy!" I couldn't contain my emotion. My little goosie had heard my call, though he had been unable to see me while I was in the woods calling him. He was on the golf course separated from the other geese by probably a

Bandy

hundred yards. When I resurfaced from the woods and stood by the other geese he saw me from afar off and came flying. There he was, my little peg-leg friend, sitting at my feet. Dreams really do come true! I was wearing a waist pack full of cracked corn which I began to mete out to him. He munched happily as I inched up beside him and petted his back, then I arched my arm over him to protect him from any jealous onlookers who might have a hankering to pull his feathers and take his corn.

"You made it, Bandy. I knew you had it in you. You're very brave and determined. It's so good to see you. I've missed you so much!" And, yes, I cried and I cried.

He answered not a word as he shoveled the corn into his bill, but I knew he was happy to see me, too. Woman and goose were reunited.

I stayed with him for a while until the sun's light was fading, then said my goodbyes. I got up and turned to walk away, then, glancing over my shoulder, I said, "You've got good taste, Bandy."

* * *

"You'll never guess who I just spent time with," I told Jesse, as I walked in noticeably late to cook supper.

"Bandy?"

"Bandy! I found him on the golf course. I petted him and he sat with me for the last twenty minutes."

Jesse stared in near disbelief. "I guess God answered your prayer. Praise the Lord!"

FIFTEEN

The Green, Green Grass of Home

Though our geese don't fly south for the winter, it seems that it's programmed into their brains to have more than one home, depending on the season. Or maybe they're just following the food sources. Ocean Edge's grass, admittedly, is greener than ours at the end of September. When I realized how close they were to their spring and summer home, I found it bewildering that they never *once* visit between August and March. Not even remembrances of cracked corn can draw them back, evidently.

Over the next few days I visited the golf course regularly. It so happened that the access driveway to my parking spot behind the cafe was on the left before the guard booth so I didn't actually have to drive up to the booth or speak to any guards before visiting my goose. That was a big break. Out of five visits, the geese were there four times, the last being on a Sunday afternoon.

The following Monday morning I got up and raised the shade and to my amazement, there was Bandy in my backyard with sixteen other geese! He had not been here in two months and had never before been here this time of year. It was clear that my visits jogged his memory of home, and though now he was often found on the outskirts of a gaggle instead of being one of the crowd, he had somehow rallied the rest of the geese to come with him. I ran out in my pajamas to say hi and I brought him some corn in a small pan from Jesse's mess kit. I did that on a whim because I had never seen him eat out of a container. I set it before him and he began jabbing at it with his bill. "You're eating from a pan! You must've learned that at Wild Care!" I said. And indeed, he did.

The geese were still in the yard when we arrived home from work. I hoped that Bandy would stay close to the house longer than the others, as he was wont to do, so that I could feed him and not them. Of all the geese, he was the one closest to the slider. I squatted there watching him. He had his eyes on me and I thought we were both just waiting for the moment when the rest would take off. Then Bandy did something unusual. A couple of geese started with the "time to go" sounds, that are sort of like a pensive person saying, "Hummm... ," only with a Kermit the frog quality of voice. Bandy suddenly shot a glance behind him and, almost in a panic, he took off towards the pond. It took the rest of the geese several minutes before they were actually ready to fly to the water. His actions were self-explanatory. Poor Bandy! He was used to being a leader

Bandy

and wanted desperately to at least be a part of the group. He didn't like lagging behind, so he was determined that that was not going to happen. He probably hoped the other geese would follow him, but they didn't. It was an awkward move. My heart went out to my goose and broke for his misfortune. Losing his foot did a number on his social life, though he tried to act as if everything was copacetic.

* * *

It was great having Bandy in the yard again, but I wasn't so sure I wanted sixteen of them at the back door. I wasn't about to complain, though. I stopped home as frequently as possible throughout the work day to visit my friend as he paddled around the pond. He was still there on Tuesday... still there on Wednesday. My mother-in-law told me he would stay on the pond during the day while the others came up to graze. At the end of the day when we drove in he came up to the sound of our car driving in over the long stone driveway. This was entirely familiar.

On Wednesday at 4:45 we drove in and, like clockwork, Bandy came hopping and flapping his way up the backyard. I brought him some treats, checked the ground for anything untoward, then sat down with him. I watched for predators as Bindy used to do while he ate. I stayed there for a full forty-five minutes and he made no move to go anywhere. When I began to feel the evening dampness I got up and said farewell, but Bandy stayed for over another hour. I watched him as he commenced his rhythmic head throwing, honking ritual, then he took to the air. That was the end of his extraordinary unseasonal three day visit.

"*Pet Goose*"—*Bandy and Marcia chilling out*

SIXTEEN

The Way is Never Long

Over the next two weeks I continued my visits to the golf course after golfing hours. I found that the geese were most often about a hundred yards down the green, about where Bandy had most likely flown from on that first night I encountered him at Ocean Edge. One afternoon when I arrived, Bandy was standing all alone on the first little corner of grass at the entrance, while the other geese were far away. It appeared he was awaiting my arrival and hoping for a treat, which I had handy.

During my earliest visits when Bandy was separate from the other geese, they had no clue what I was doing with him. Consequently, they ignored us, except for two geese who came waddling with haste out of the crowd. They came to yank feathers and steal a meal, and to my amazement, they were Bindy and 338. Among all the people that I'm sure made a transit through that golf course, they recognized me as readily as Bandy did, and from a distance. I had to give them appeasement rations so he could eat in peace.

The day after I'd found Bandy waiting for me at the entrance, I arrived to spot him a great distance down the fairway with the gaggle. He immediately spotted and recognized me. I ducked behind a large rock that was on the edge of the green to hide from the others, then I peeked out and waved. Bandy came flying to meet me. He never ceased to astound me. The only explanation for his vigilant response is that he was waiting and watching for me.

It was a pleasure to observe my goose's ever increasing aptitude with his stump. During his absence it had healed over nicely and it was black like the rest of his leg instead of pink and raw in appearance. He was now hobbling along like a peg-leg pirate and flapping less to get around.

One day as I was driving along the road leading into the complex, I saw my dentist, who lived at Ocean Edge, taking a walk. He was a friend of Jesse's and mine. He had been to our house and knew about the geese, so I told him what I was doing there.

Being from Taiwan with high-rise apartments and a dense concentration of people, Dr. Chung had been impressed with the acreage surrounding our house, and the stories of wildlife. "It's like you have your own national park," he observed. That was a slight exaggeration. He actually got to see and hear a fledging red-tailed hawk in our backyard. It was apparently crying out to its mother for some supplemental feedings, in a voice that sounded, to me, like a seagull with a sore throat. A fox or coyote sighting would have been nice, but we were glad there was at least something to back up our claims of wildlife sightings.

The first time I met Andy Chung, he had taken over my retired dentist's office. When I went for a long overdue routine checkup I noticed that the office had been refurbished. Part of the new look was an unusual symbol inlaid in the shiny wooden floor. It was a lotus flower, but instead of a Buddha seated above it, there was a cross. "Are you a Christian?" I asked the diminutive, gentle young dentist. He was actually my husband's age, but seemed much younger.

"Yes, I am," he obliged. His manner was friendly and I instantly knew that he was like-minded, and someone I could be friends with. I also sensed that he was on the shy side and could probably use a few friends who shared his faith. I wanted to introduce him to Jesse, who tends to avoid dentist visits, but has enviable teeth nonetheless.

It took about a year and a half of appointments, route canals and crowns, but finally I invited him over for supper and a movie. He had just returned from a trip to his native Taiwan and he came bearing a hostess gift. It was Taiwanese snack food for our munching pleasure. One package was freeze-dried squid and the other was some kind of dried soy product. As I remember, it looked like a bunch of big black prunes in a package with all the air sucked out of it. I couldn't tell the exact ingredients because all of the print on both package labels was in Chinese, but it doesn't matter because I'm allergic to mold and chemicals and couldn't have eaten it anyway. Jesse was about to take some church members and their kids on a camping trip to the White Mountains and he planned to give the munchies as game prizes just to freak people out. I set the sealed packages on my bed while I dialed up my sister to tell her about the novel hostess gift. The second I turned my back, the cat appeared and dug into the squid. With little bite holes in the packaging, it was no longer a viable game prize. At least somebody really liked it.

Jesse and Dr. Chung hit it off great, and between Christian and computer topics, they had plenty to talk about. I was happy to have made friends with my dentist.

On this particular evening at Ocean Edge when I saw Andy walking, I put the window down and called out, "Dr. Chung!" He came over to the car.

"I'm about to go see my one-footed goose," I explained.

"Can I come, too?" he asked.

"Sure. Hop in."

I told Dr. Chung that Bandy lived six months in my backyard and the other six months in his backyard, at the fifth hole.

We pulled up in the parking lot then moseyed down to the grazing flock. I found Bandy in pretty close proximity to the other geese, who were beginning to catch on that I was bringing treats to Bandy. I was glad to have some help keeping them at bay. Dr. Chung may not have been a natural with the geese, but he quickly learned the art of weilding a sand-trap rake to ward off would-be swipers while Bandy got some corn. I found that my dentist was brave about more than snacking on freeze-dried squid!

Bandy

* * *

After three weeks of visiting Ocean Edge, there began to be a nip in the air that declared fall had set in and winter was on its way. One day I stopped at the golf course and there were no geese to be found. As I was leaving I heard the distant honking of geese and there high up in the sky was a V-formation flying in a southeasterly direction. I wondered if it was Bandy's group being compelled by the temperatures to seek a warmer climate. Just when I thought I was privy to his dependable whereabouts, he came no more. Each subsequent visit turned up no geese, until I finally decided to save the gas and ditch the futile trips.

Prior to the holidays I caught a cold that went into my chest. We had to whittle our Thanksgiving dinner plans to a dinner for three, since I'm the one who does all the cooking. Even by Christmas time I was still feeling exhausted so I opted out of cooking the make-up meal for Jesse's Manhattan brother and his German wife and we instead got Chinese food to go.

All during that bout with sickness I would've been too out of it to be visiting geese, but come Christmas I missed Bandy and decided to take a drive to the golf course. On this unseasonably warm day I went with gift in hand and checked out a deserted fairway. I did the same on New Year's Day. No Bandy. No geese.

On January eighth I decided to check one more time and there on Sol's Pond, which is also on the premises, were about fifty geese. I stood before the pond and blew my goose call. Nobody made a move. I blew again. Unable to conjure up

Bandy, I left.

The next morning at seven o' clock my husband shook me awake. "Guess who's in the backyard."

"A deer?"

"Go look."

Fully expecting to see a deer, I looked out from a third story window without my glasses. Down below I saw a little black and white blur. "A *skunk*?" I asked in disgust that Jesse had awakened me for such an unexciting sighting.

"No. It's Bandy!"

"You're kidding!" I said, knowing a visit like this just doesn't happen in January.

He wasn't kidding. Bandy had come all alone. This time, I hadn't seen him in three months. It is my feeling that he was one of the fifty geese on Sol's Pond when I blew the goose call the day before. He knew it was me and for whatever reason, perhaps peer pressure, he hadn't responded. He was feeling almost obligated not to leave me in the dark as to his whereabouts, so he showed up at my back door at daybreak. We were at the very outset of the harshest deep freeze that Cape Cod has ever seen since I've been on the planet, so I was glad for a day to fatten him up in anticipation of the Arctic blast. I had, not one day with him, but two, during which time he pigged out on a rich buffet of multigrain and seed bread from the health food store and some cracked corn. I actually postponed my last job of that Friday so I could spend time with him. He had a wonderful and filling day, then flew off into a backdrop of deepening violet hues, echoing resounding honks like nostalgic poetry.

Bandy

* * *

Two days later Jesse and I were on our way to church. As we traveled Route 124, picturesque for all of its ponds that can be easily viewed from the winding highway, several geese caught my eye huddled along the edge of Long Pond. Though it was mostly frozen, there was some open water to serve as a food source and hydration for them, and a means of shelter from predators. "I'd like to stop there on the way home," I told Jesse.

After a trip to the natural food market, and bearing loaves of healthy grain and seed bread, we stopped at Long Pond, which is on the Harwich-Brewster line, about two miles from our house. For lack of anywhere else to park, Jesse pulled into a zone where parking is prohibited, so he stayed with the car feeling a little antsy. As I crossed over the bike path with eyes fixed on the waterfowl, who should I spot first, but Bandy! He was standing on the ice while the rest of the geese were in the water. He recognized me right away, eased himself down into the water and paddled over. As I tossed bread out to him the other geese swam away, though I did draw some ducks which were probably summer residents of our Griffith's Pond. I didn't want to keep Jesse waiting too long so I decided to drop him off at home and return alone.

On my second visit to Long Pond in one day, I stood at the water's edge and called out to Bandy. Just then a man who was walking his dog along the bike path came nearby. Feeling like I owed an explanation to this man as to why I was speaking out to the waterfowl, I stated, "One of these geese lives in my yard half of the year." Positive that he was now wondering how I could be so sure that I knew one of these clones, I explained further to this complete stranger, "He only has one foot and I saw him earlier standing on the ice over there."

He seemed friendly enough so I offered some more information. "These geese shouldn't even be here in such frigid weather. Flying south has been bred out of them by us. They are the distant offspring of live decoys, so generations of them never learned from their ancestors to fly south." I spoke of how waterfowl hunting was big on Cape Cod in days gone by.

"You see that place with the white barn across the pond?" the man asked. "That's where I live. It belonged to my grandfather. It was a *duck hunting farm*."

Happy that my dissertation about waterfowl hunting didn't meet with complete disinterest, we continued the conversation.

"You should've seen when I moved in—the barn was just *full* of old hand-carved decoys, blinds, things like that. Unfortunately, I threw them all out."

"Ouch!" I empathized over his former ignorance of the fortune in old decoys that he had tossed away.

By now Bandy had come over to me and the stranger could see that there really was a goose that knew me among the many pond dwellers. Bandy was leery, though, of the dog's keen interest in him. Then the man and his dog moved on. I stayed a few more minutes pondering what the geese might do once the last of the open pond water froze, which, in light of the forecast, could be any day.

Jesse and I passed by again on our way to the Sunday evening church service. We could see the geese and ducks huddling in the icy cold in a reduced aperture of open water. We stopped again

Bandy

on our way home, and though this time the darkness obscured the sight of Bandy, I summoned him with my goose call. Among the prolific quacks of ducks came a sole honking voice. He knew it was me, and though he was not comfortable leaving the small water hole in the dark, he wanted me to know it was him.

"Cold, Cold World"—Bandy sits alone on the frozen pond, waiting for the urge to fly away and rejoin his group

Bandy's "footprints"

SEVENTEEN

That Old North Wind

One day after finding Bandy two miles away at Long Pond Jesse and I stopped home for lunch. "Bandy!" Jesse shouted with surprise as we walked from the garage into the house. Bandy had come for another visit, apparently because I had called him the night before and he had been unable to come to me. There he was standing right at the back door. Closer examination revealed that someone had fed him. Before him was a pile of corn and a metal pan of water. He donned a corn mustache and there was corn in the water, so we knew that he had partaken of both.

My mother-in-law was hosting bridge upstairs when she and her friends had noticed Bandy in the yard all alone. Her friend Shirley Sarles, an avid birder, knew what he came for and, at my mother-in-law's suggestion, decided to help him out. The ground was now completely frozen, as were most of the ponds, and there was a snow cover of an inch or so. Food was scarce.

We hated to leave him to go back to work, but when we returned home at 4:30 he was still just inches from the back door. Knowing that we were about to get slammed with some North Pole weather, I was wishing I could invite him in and give him a drawn bath to sleep in.

I stepped outside and squatted beside him. He looked healthy and beautiful despite the gash of missing feathers on the right side of his neck. It had been that way for nearly a year due to his harsh footless scratching apparatus on that side. Bundled up like a woolly mammoth, I ignored the fact that the temperature was starting to dip into the teens.

"Hummm," Bandy began the conversation. "Hummm," I parroted. "Hummm, hummm," he said. "Hummm, hummm," I replied. "Hummm, hummm, hummm," he mused, in a voice reminiscent of Kermit the frog. I emulated his tone. "Hummm, hummm, hummm," I said to my friend, hoping that he could understand, because I surely couldn't. And so the conversation went for several minutes.

Knowing that I would most likely witness his departure, I had my camera with me, which was now poised at my eye. He began conveying body language that spurred me to prepare to snap a picture of my favorite bird taking flight, something I had never done before. I wondered if it would be the last time I might see him. Could a handicapped goose that's supposed to fly south survive the weather that was forecast? Just then, he turned, and in a split second he was honking and taking to the

Bandy

air as I stood in the cold and watched. Then, in spite of the evening's dimming light, I noticed that my friend had left his tracks in the thin layer of snow. They consisted of the imprint of a left turned-in webbed foot and the drag of a peg-leg that looked like a backwards "C", a foot and a peg-leg. I had the thought that now, in the snow, I would be able to tell if he had been somewhere by his unique "footprints".

The next few nights were brutal, weather-wise. One night it actually dipped down to minus six but the stiff winds made it feel like thirty below zero. This trend went on and on. Arctic weather is an anomaly on Cape Cod and I was sure our geese had never experienced the likes of it. Long Pond, though reaching depths of 60 feet, was totally frozen over now and the waterfowl were gone. I searched for them on weekends but the only geese I found were on the south side of the Cape and Bandy wasn't among them. They were huddled in a tidal river that flows in and out from Nantucket Sound. Most of the river was frozen. Even the bay on the north side of Cape Cod was frozen as far as the eye could see. Wild Care was flooded with patients, like sea birds that were grounded and don't have the wherewithal to take flight from land. Birds were brought to the facility that were frostbitten, starving, and exhausted.

How were the waterfowl going to eat? How could they sleep and be safe from predators? I was even reading about dogs requiring rescue from the freezing water after going into the tidal river in pursuit of the geese and ducks huddled there. Then there was the account told to me of a deer that was chased by a pack of coyotes onto Upper Mill Pond. Once on the ice, it lost its footing, and consequently, its life. For the coyotes, it was several days' dinner kept nicely on ice. There was also a newspaper account of harbor seals out at Monomoy sunning themselves on the ice. Many of them were taken as they became easy prey for the coyotes. The ice was obviously making everything more vulnerable to predators.

I was convinced now that our Cape Cod geese did not fly south, period. After all, I saw them on Long Pond right up until the first few days of being plunged into the deep freeze. There would be no flying around now. It was savage and the wind was as merciless as the temperatures.

After weeks of weather adverse to everything living outdoors, we began to experience some daytime temperatures above the freezing mark. I went on a Saturday to check Long Pond, which is aptly named for its length of over two miles. There wasn't a goose to be found. Instead, I saw around thirty ice sailors speeding across the ice in their crafts, which looked like small Sunfish sailboats on skate blades. They appeared to be going about fifty or sixty miles per hour. Any prior knowledge of this sport had somehow completely evaded me, so the sight I was beholding came as a surprise. It was like an ice sailing party. I marveled that they weren't all crashing into each other, they were moving at such a clip. I surmised that the ice must be pretty thick to support all that weight and that it wouldn't be thawing any time soon.

Several days later I checked Long Pond and noticed a half dozen waterfowl sitting in a break in the ice that appeared to run the width of the pond. I wondered if it had been produced by the weight of the ice sailors and their crafts, who were still at it. Through my binoculars I determined that the waterfowl were

Bandy

geese, but that they were too far away from land on any side to be approachable. I began checking for them with regularity as the ice melted bit by bit.

* * *

Two more weeks passed and finally I spotted a large group of geese, around fifty, on Hinckley's Pond, which was now displaying a sizable area of open water. This had to be Bandy's group, since Hinckley's Pond is along route 124, very close to Long Pond. Tortured by the duration of Bandy's absence during such a bitter spell, I coerced my husband to pull into the tiny parking lot overlooking the pond to search for him.

"Don't be long," he admonished, in light of the fact that we had to do a few things at home, including popping a bag of concealable microwave popcorn, then travel back to Harwich for a four o' clock movie. It was already quarter of three and my husband likes to be early for everything.

I stood at the water's edge and blew my goose call. Jesse soon joined me and we began peering through binoculars at some of the geese that were standing on the ice out towards the middle of this considerably smaller pond. There was a goose standing on one leg. It was ignoring me, even to the point of turning its head backwards and burying its bill between its wings as if taking a snooze. How a bird could sleep while balancing on one leg is beyond me, but equally puzzling was the prospect of Bandy ignoring me.

"Why doesn't it come?" I decided it must not be Bandy. Geese sometimes hang out standing on one leg even if they have two. I've been fooled by many a goose into thinking I saw Bandy until the retracted leg was finally lowered.

Suddenly Jesse's attention was drawn to a red and white seaplane at a private residence that overlooked the pond. It was parked on the sand like a docked boat, a seemingly strange place to see an aircraft.

"I noticed it yesterday. Come down this little path and you can get a better look," I said. Jesse began following me, then stopped short with a gasp that made me pivot.

"What's this? Is it a goose?" he asked, holding up a large wing he'd found just to the side of the path. It looked like fresh kill.

"Bandy! He's the one a coyote would stalk because of his distance from the rest of the flock. He's probably had to sleep on the ice."

I started searching for the rest of the remains.

"Here's another wing!" I exclaimed, turning the severed body part with a stick.

"Come on, we have to go, *now*," Jesse reminded me with consternation in his voice.

On the way home I couldn't hold back the tears. "If Bandy doesn't show up in the yard tomorrow, I'll be convinced that was him."

We rushed through our preparation to go out again, then raced to the movie theater, only to have to sit through twenty minutes of previews being projected on the screen before a nearly empty house. The fact that we were there to see *The Passion of The Christ* made me feel better about walking in with red nose and eyes, then frequently dabbing and blowing throughout the movie. I felt miserable! How could my goose's life have ended so treacherously? And, by comparison, what I was witnessing on the screen made me feel badly for being this upset about a goose. The dual thoughts of Christ being snuffed out for my sins, and Bandy being snuffed out for no good reason at all were almost too much to contemplate in one sitting.

EIGHTEEN

CSI: Harwich

The next day as soon as we got home from work, I went out again and headed in the direction of Hinckley's Pond. I was determined to further examine the carnage on the path to see if there were any legs at the scene, expressly, a footless one. Upon arriving, I maneuvered my way down the steep, wooded hill from the parking lot to the water and sounded several honks on the goose call. It was an identical scenario to the previous day: fifty geese, a goose standing on one leg on the ice, no one responding to my call. The only difference was, I saw the one-legged goose put his other leg down. How disappointing!

Next, I proceeded gingerly towards the crime scene. There it was, as grisly as I had remembered it. I readied the latex gloves, grabbed a stick, and started turning things over. Then I came across a sight still indelible in my mind. Along with the rest of the discarded bird was an intact head. To my surprise, it wasn't a goose at all! It was a hawk, of all things. The sharp, curved mandible was unmistakable. Who on earth would do this to a hawk?

Chagrinned at my behavior from the previous day, but relieved that the carnage wasn't Bandy, I turned to leave. Then something caught my attention out on the ice. What was a small dog doing on the ice when the whole perimeter of the pond was melted for several yards. I panicked. I grabbed my binoculars and focused. This was no dog. Instead I was viewing a huge otter. I had never in my life seen an otter in the wild and didn't know they existed in ponds. I had heard of sea otters and river otters, but never a pond otter. There it was. Now I had not only seen a hawk that I thought was a goose, but an otter that I thought was a dog. I was coming to the conclusion that I need my glasses for more than driving. I watched the otter for a while until it slipped off the ice and disappeared into the water.

Well, Bandy hadn't been murdered, at least not at Hinckley's Pond on this side, on this day. I didn't know whether to take comfort in that thought. After all, he should be with all the other geese if he were alive. And if he had heard me, why hadn't he come? Hadn't he always felt morally obligated to present himself at my door if I was looking for him, just so I wouldn't worry?

That next Sunday at the end of our church service, two friends were discussing their reactions to *The Passion*. "I cried so much during that movie," Vicky said.

"I only cried *once*," Flo responded, "from the time the movie started till the time it ended!"

"Well, I was crying on the way *in* to the movie theater," I chimed in. Their response of laughter made me realize that they thought I was trying to one up them. I had to explain that my emotional display was not a movie review.

NINETEEN

A Day in the Life

Two more weeks went by with no sign of Bandy. He was supposed to have come around the last day of February and here it was, the middle of March. What's worse, geese started coming back to our pond and none of them was you-know-who. The first to show up was not a goose I knew, but I believe he was here for two days during mid-October when Bandy came and brought fifteen geese with him. At that time there was an unfamiliar goose with very defined white eyebrows, unlike Osama's scattered eyebrows. This new goose was shy, and definitely not a grouch, but his eyebrows earned him the name "Groucho". He was with us for a few days until a man hired to do some yard work scared him away with his chain saw.

The next goose to arrive flew in to our Snow Pond, a small,

shallow weed-choked pond, termed by the realtor a "viewing pond". In other words, "Look, but don't go in it." I was downstairs and heard the second goose honking overhead, so I grabbed the goose call, opened the slider, and answered him before he even landed. Then I followed him to the place where he came in for a landing. Eager to see who he was, I carefully descended the hill to Snow Pond, bearing corn. Snow Pond is surrounded by woods, bushes, and brambles and the only easily accessible portion of it was still frozen. Although this pond is probably only knee deep, I didn't dare to walk on the ice, but I was able to draw this goose up onto the frozen surface by tossing some corn. "He knows me," I thought. The next thing I noticed as he approached was that he was banded. "Let's see, if it's 338 alone, that means Bindy didn't make it. That would be very sad," I said out loud to myself as the goose moved closer. I ran back to the house for my binoculars so I could read his number.

With building suspense, I focused on the band: "0958-79755". No way! It was Father Goose! Alone!

I never thought I'd feel sad for Father Goose, but it was kind of pitiful to see him all alone on the tiny half-frozen pond. How things change! Mother Goose evidently didn't survive the harsh winter and the goslings were probably making lives for themselves.

Before long Groucho came back. By observing interactions between the two geese, it became clear that it wasn't family size that made Father Goose obnoxious. It was just the fabric of his personality. He was boorish to poor Groucho even though it was only the two of them. I guess he didn't care to have any friends. He would hiss and maneuver his neck in a snakelike fashion, then charge at his only would-be company. Unlike Osama, he hadn't changed a bit in spite of his loss. No wonder, of the two, I favored Groucho.

Two weeks into March on a Friday morning I was puttering about the downstairs, which was once a bar and game room, but now served as our main living space. Since we don't drink and don't party, apart from the occasional church get-together, the bar became the breakfast bar. In the place of the previous owner's pool table we had our dining room table, right in front of the slider where we could view and have quick access to all that the backyard proffered us.

Overhead I could hear some honking. I looked out and caught sight of three geese clearing the treetops, then dropping to Griffith's Pond. Of course, I had to go down and see who it was. There appeared to be a mated pair and one other goose. While I was trying to figure them out, a fourth goose came honking towards the pond. I took out my goose call and answered his honks. As he landed, two of the new additions swam at him in attack mode and chased him towards the other side. Then I got a better look at one of the attackers and he was wearing a little clown mask! It was the white-faced goose with the black cap, orange legs and colorful bill who visited one day a year ago. Back then I gave him the name "Buddy" because he was friendly, but he had only stuck around for a few hours. Now here he was with a normal Canada goose and they were obviously an item. I hoped they would stay and produce some goslings that might give us a hint as to his ancestry. He absorbed my attention for a while, then I noticed Groucho mounting our neighbor's dock. He had been back and forth between our pond and some other retreat over the past two weeks. I assumed he was the one who flew in alone and was attacked. Still no Bandy.

Happy to have been there to greet all the geese, but sad that Bandy, who had always come back first, was still absent, I ambled back to the house. My feeling that he hadn't survived was beginning to cement with each additional goose that flew in to the pond only to turn out not to be him. It was so disappointing!

Another day on Griffith's Pond had come and gone. My hope was fading. I had to keep reminding myself that I had not yet seen Bindy, 338, or Osama either.

* * *

On Saturday morning I told Jesse my plan was to spend some time searching for Bandy on the local waterways. Before leaving I went down to say hello to Groucho and Father Goose. The little clown goose and his girlfriend had left before day's end the previous day so we were back down to two geese. First to greet me was Groucho. Not far behind him was who I thought would be Father Goose, but the attitude was different. This goose was docile. As I scrutinized his features I noticed some of the black feathers were missing from his neck, giving him a scruffy appearance. "Is that *Bandy?*" I asked aloud. The goose swam closer, then used his little stump to pull himself up onto the shore. "It *is* you! Oh, Bandy, I can't believe it's you!"

Like a family member greeting a soldier who has just stepped on home turf after being on the battlefront, my emotions soared. This little handicapped wildling had weathered the storm. Not

Bandy

only the literal battery of the elements, but he had weathered so many storms in his decade of years, particularly this last one.

"You're a survivor, Bandy. You're a *true survivor*."

It took a while to dawn on me, but I believe now that Bandy was the goose that flew in on Friday morning and was attacked as he landed. I think he swam to goose point and spent the night there. The reason I believe this is because a total of four geese came Friday and I only accounted for Buddy, his girlfriend, and Groucho. There definitely had been a fourth goose that I lost track of because of my fixation on the arrival of the little clown goose. And if that was Bandy that flew in alone, I find a strange solace in the fact I was standing on the shore blowing the goose call as he made his entrance back into my life. I hope he can somehow understand that I was waiting in great anticipation of that moment, even though it somehow snuck right past me.

* * *

And now, at the conclusion of the recounting of Bandy's story, all is happy on the home front. Whether it happens to be at noon or late afternoon, when he hears our car drive in, he immediately comes up to the house. Aside from a few run-ins with Father Goose and an episode of being closely trailed at a clip by a swan from one side of the pond to the other, Bandy is peaceful and contented. He seemed to hit it off well with Groucho and spent one whole day hanging out with him on the lawn, then when the time came, they took off together and landed together in the middle of the pond. Groucho's away right now, but I know Bandy will find more friends when someone other than Father Goose is resident. He is at peace with himself and I hope that I can be a contributing factor to his sense of well-being. He knows I'm on his side.

TWENTY

A Honker for a Tutor

During the time that I have been privileged to live here and have Bandy for a friend, my observances of him have taught me a few things. I actually faced situations recently where thoughts of my friend gave me courage to go forward.

The first thing I've observed in Bandy is his lack of malice. On May 15th, two months after Bandy came back, 338 returned without Bindy. She has always summered here, so her absence leads me to believe she either didn't survive the winter, or she's being fickle again. Do geese hold grudges? Maybe not. At least, not Bandy. He welcomed 338 with an open heart. Never mind what 338 did in the past. The past is behind them. They are best of friends again, swimming together and hanging out at goose point. I never see one without the other. Bandy could be missing out on the joy of companionship if he decided to hold a grudge.

The longtime friends, banded on the same day in 1995, are pals again.

There is one goose, though, that Bandy avoids, and with good reason. One morning when Bandy was alone on the pond, I was feeding him some corn at the shore, when suddenly he began acting fearful. He pulled away, searching for a place to hide. I looked around and saw nothing amiss, but then moments later I heard distant honking. Geese have excellent hearing and know each other's voices. As Father Goose was coming in for a landing, I looked back at Bandy. He had moved down the shoreline over by some bushes. His neck was stretched out level with the ground and he was staying perfectly still, in hopes that he would be invisible. Well, Father Goose saw him anyway, but Bandy had the right idea. "A prudent man [goose] foresees the evil and hides himself, but the simple pass on and are punished (with suffering)." Proverbs 22:3 The Amplified Bible

The latter part of the proverb brings another incident to mind. Recently 338 came to get some corn. Father Goose was nearby and decided to attack 338. I was powerless to stop him as he climbed on 338's back and was apparently trying to drown him. Father Goose was moving across the water effortlessly, as if riding the back of a turtle, only his mode of transportation was a helpless goose underwater. Every time 338 lifted his head up for air, the menacing Father Goose pushed it back under, with seeming murderous intent. What seemed like thirty seconds went by before 338 was able to shed his rider and surface for air. A little prudence and avoidance could have spared him such punishment. Bandy, on the other hand, would rather pass up corn than put himself in harm's way.

Besides some good goose sense, (whoever coined the term "silly goose"?) another thing I observe in Bandy is perseverance. I personally haven't suffered to the extent of losing a limb, being carried by sickness to the brink of death, or losing my mate to my best friend, all of which Bandy has suffered. But I have had situations that, though they pale in comparison to some of the above mentioned scenarios, have frustrated and inconvenienced my daily existence. We all have them. My recent problems had to do with carpal tunnel, frozen shoulder, and great difficulty writing. In the midst of it all, eight chapters of Bandy's story got accidentally deleted from the computer—as in, edited away irretrievably. Poof! At the time, I did what any mature adult would do. I buried my head in my bedding and cried. This is when I began to think about Bandy and how hard everyday activities must be for him. He just keeps plugging away. He never gives up no matter how discouraging his circumstances become. He is patient in all his troubles, and he never complains.

With my husband's help, I was able to restore my work in about three weeks. It was a setback, but it wasn't the end of the world. I didn't understand why it had happened, but I had to guess it was meant to teach me something. Like patience and perseverance.

* * *

Bandy has, for ten or eleven years, avoided hunters' bullets, coyotes' jaws, and the grasp of at least one fox two days in a row.

He survived the bone-chilling grip of a fierce North Pole winter that didn't want to let go. He has snubbed the rejection of his peers and even that of his lifetime mate. Though the hand of fate has dealt him a couple of debilitating blows, this goose is tough, this goose is smart, this goose is savvy. He may have to work twice as hard as every other goose to socialize, get food, and keep his balance, but he is doing it. He refuses to allow his misfortune to cause him to fold his wings and shrink in self-pity.

When I had thought that he was depressed last summer, the truth was that he was a very sick goose with a raging infection, like in my dream. It wasn't his confidence, but rather, his very life that was ebbing away. I just have to contemplate that I'm glad he was on this pond when it happened, and not someplace where he might have been overlooked.

To observe him munching happily twelve inches from a swan and in the presence of Father Goose, one can safely ascertain that his handicap is physical, only. It has not encroached upon on his attitude or his outlook. It has not crippled his life. The fact that I now wield a large stick may aid Bandy's sense of security. He understands what the stick is for and isn't threatened by it, but the geese with ill will are. I never use it on anyone, but I look pretty authoritative, and always hope that the neighbors don't see me.

My goose now has a venue to speak to all those who will take the time to listen with their hearts. In spite of his many tragedies, he doesn't think his life is all that bad. Consider him as he confidently comes to my door for his bowl, sits in the sun, and nourishes himself as I watch for predators (and Father Goose). He has found a friend who is one hundred percent *for* him, and delights in him—one who will even go searching for him just to treat him.

As a result, the fifteen other geese that have taken up residence on the pond this season (eleven adults and four goslings) all watch Bandy. They follow him everywhere he goes, hoping to get a piece of the action. I guess that makes him the leader once again. Life is good.

In conclusion, take a lesson from Bandy. If life throws you a curve ball and you suddenly find yourself in the recesses of loneliness, sickness or despair, don't lose heart. It may be you are about to find a friend in higher places. That friend may even be One who has answered many a prayer on behalf of a goose.

*Not one sparrow can fall to the ground without
your Father knowing it.
And the very hairs of your head are all numbered.
So don't worry!
You are more valuable to Him than many sparrows.*

Matthew 10:29-31
The Living Bible

"Faithful Friends"—Photo by *Stephanie Foster*/The Cape Codder

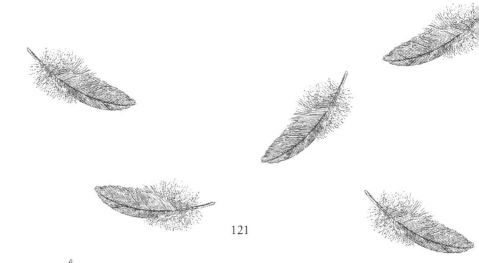

More Photos from the Goose Gallery

Tux with his brood, recently hatched on our pond

"Bird in the Hand"—Photo by Jane Frances Ditzel

This book would not be complete if I failed to tell you about Sprout. She showed up this past spring, all wound up and running around the yard like she owned the place. This crazed little goose with the huge eyes and skinny neck came running at high speed to our back door. I opened it and stuck my hand out to greet her, and she bit it! (Goose bites don't hurt, by the way.) After a good belly-laugh, I offered her a handful of corn. She began eating it, right out of my hand! No other goose had ever done that—not even Bandy. I concluded she must be Father Goose's kid, which would be enough to make anyone crazy. I was there the day she hatched the previous summer, so she thought it quite natural to interact with me. My suspicions were confirmed when Sprout and her boyfriend, Turkey, became the constant companions of Father Goose and his mate. And to think, I once dreaded the prospect of Father Goose's full-grown procreations! She's a little peach, and Father Goose's one redeeming quality.

"Got Corn?"—The lovely Sprout

For more pictures, visit Bandy's website at:
www.bandys.net or www.bandythegoose.com

Acknowledgments

I owe a debt of gratitude to Bob Tarte, author of *Enslaved by Ducks*, for his willingness to offer not only editing, but guidance and encouragement throughout the process of writing this book.

Special thanks to my North Carolina friends, Ed McBride and Clydine Kime for their assistance with the Lockhart Gaddy story. Thanks to Bill McClennan who first shared it with me. Also to North Carolinian, Fletch Good, my cover designer, who shares with us a special love for geese. He came to us through the providence of a one-footed Canada goose in his area and the help of the google search engine.

Thanks to my husband, Jesse, for all of his labor on the computer, his suggestions and help in countless ways, and for believing in me.

Unending thanks to Lela Larned for her dedication to Cape Cod's critters and for saving Bandy's life.

Thanks to Terri Fox for her suggestions.

I will forever appreciate Dr. Russell K. Pier, founding president of Faith School of Theology, who not only taught me the principles of faith and prayer, but also showed me with his life that when we dare to believe, miracles really do happen!

I am grateful to my sister, Sheila Galvin, the walking thesaurus, for her help each time I lacked the right word. I also appreciate her example of faith while enduring more afflictions and hardships than one person should have.

A word of thanks to my old high school guidance couselor-turned-children's author, Dick Wainwright, for his generosity with information and his offers to help in so many ways.

Thanks to H.W. Heussman for always being willing to give his time in sharing from his storehouse of information on geese.

Thanks to all of the folks who said, "You should write a book about that," when they heard Bandy's story. And I can't fail to mention the good people who live on the cul-de-sac across the pond, ie., Becky and Dave, and their neighbors, who have seen me all too often, trekking through to check on my goose.

Diane Maurino, owner of The Book Rack, deserves accolades for her years of dedication to our feathered friends. The former New Yorker preceded me as "the goose lady". She even chopped the pond ice for them in winter. She once told me that she could never live on a pond again because being involved in the lives of geese was "too painful". Now, how's that for a goose lover? This is definitely a woman who understands.

As is Stephanie Foster. She wrote the feature newspaper story about Bandy and me for the Cape Codder, for which I am grateful. She also once wrote a magazine article called, "Never Love a Goose". (The problem is, once you get attached, they fly away!)

Thank you to all who read this book.

Last but not least, an enormous thank you to my mother-in-law, Ginger Shaffer, for providing us with an idyllic place to live. Without her I would not have met Bandy and this story would not have happened.

Much praise to God, who did all of the working behind the scenes.

A graduate of Faith School of Theology in Maine, Marcia Croce Martin is a speaker, artist and sculptor. She lives in Brewster, Massachusetts, with her husband Jesse. Her latest work in progress is an illustrated children's version of Bandy's story.

To order copies of this book,
please go to Bandythegoose.com
Email Marcia at: bandy@phenomi.net

ISBN 1-41204289-5